• Praise for •
Acting Techniques for Everyday Life

"This is a wonderfully healing, challenging book about the art of self-transformation. Jane Marla Robbins describes acting techniques and shows how they can be applied to all sorts of difficult everyday situations. I'm here to say that these exercises really work! *Acting Techniques for Everyday Life* will make you feel terrific about yourself."

—PATRICIA BOSWORTH, contributing editor for *Vanity Fair*

"Essential reading to help anyone prepare for the difficult situations in their lives. The techniques are practical and fun. It's a standing ovation for Robbins!"

—BARBARA PACHTER, author of *The Power of Positive Confrontation* and *When the Little Things Count...And They Always Count*

"As an educator, former media and film executive and producer, I think Jane Marla Robbins has developed a fabulous confidence-building tool for people from all walks of life. What an idea! This book is a classic of the self-help genre and a masterful example of the power of a great teacher."

—STEPHEN R. GREENWALD, president, Metropolitan College of New York

"Jane Marla Robbins presents excellent techniques to assist people in overcoming shyness and performance anxiety. Her suggestions for helping people be more centered, use their voices to communicate more effectively, and be more present in every way are invaluable for those lacking in self-esteem and confidence."

—STANLEY L. RUSTIN, Ph.D., Director of Counseling at Queensborough Community College

"The techniques Jane describes with such insight, depth, and humor are certainly veritable skills for success."

—ADELE SCHEELE, author of *Skills for Success* and *Jumpstart Your Career in College*

"*Acting Techniques for Everyday Life* is destined to become the classic handbook for using acting techniques to get through difficult times in your life. It's thrilling to get such empowering important information in a package full of such humor, warmth, and wisdom."

—TALIA SHIRE, actress

"I have often wondered why I haven't used my numerous acting "lifelines" in my own life. Now I know why. Because until now, no one has written a book that so brilliantly shows me how. Jane's book is a page-turner and an eye opener! With every page she has helped me open my eyes to myself!"

—LYNN REDGRAVE, actress, playwright

• About the Author •

JANE MARLA ROBBINS is thrilled to have her many years of experience as an actress, writer, and teacher come together in this book.

Jane has been teaching acting techniques for everyday life for over twenty years all over the United States—at schools, universities, in corporations, and in private practice. She currently leads workshops on Acting Techniques for Business Success in Los Angeles and teaches classes at Loyola Marymount University and the University of Judaism.

Jane was commissioned by the Kennedy Center in Washington, D.C. to write and perform the one-woman play *Reminiscences of Mozart by His Sister*, which she also performed at New York's Lincoln Center. Jane also wrote and starred in *Dear Nobody* (which ran for a year in New York, was produced on CBS, and then toured all over the United States and to London); *Jane Avril* (New York, Copenhagen); *Miriam's Dance* (New York, Los Angeles); and *Bats in the Belfry* (Spoleto Festival, Italy).

Jane has appeared in several motion pictures, including *Rocky I, Rocky II, Rocky V, Arachnophobia, True Identity,* and *Coming Apart*. Her television credits include *ER, Murder She Wrote, The Heidi Chronicles, Beverly Hills 90210, Knots Landing, Falcon Crest,* and *79 Park Avenue*. She also performed on Broadway in *Richard III* and *Morning, Noon & Night*.

A published poet and essayist, Jane graduated magna cum laude from Bryn Mawr College and studied at the Graduate School of Psychology at Antioch College. She lives outside Los Angeles, California.

ACTING Techniques for Everyday LIFE

Look and Feel
Self-Confident in Difficult
Real-Life Situations

• JANE MARLA ROBBINS •

MARLOWE & COMPANY
NEW YORK

ACTING TECHNIQUES FOR EVERYDAY LIFE:
Look and Feel Self-Confident in Difficult Real-Life Situations

Published by
Marlowe & Company
An Imprint of Avalon Publishing Group Incorporated
161 William Street, 16th Floor
New York, NY 10038

Library of Congress Cataloging-in-Publication Data
Robbins, Jane Marla.
Acting techniques for everyday life : look and feel self-confident in difficult real life situations / by Jane Marla Robbins.
p. cm.
ISBN 1-56924-554-1 (trade paper)
1. Self-confidence. 2. Acting—Psychological aspects. I. Title.
BF575.S39 R63 2002
158.2—dc21
2002141431

Designed by Pauline Neuwirth, Neuwirth & Associates, Inc.

Printed in Canada
Distributed by Publishers Group West

The names of the people who have worked with me, whose stories I share in this book, have been changed to honor their privacy.

The names of the actors I have quoted have been kept to honor their craft and their work

For my grandma Esther Robbins, who came to America from Russia in 1900 and didn't always know how to act.

And for my mother, Mildred Robbins Leet,
for teaching me how to take action,
and for her love.

• Contents •

• Introduction •

I HAVE ACTED in plays, movies, and on television for over thirty years, and while I was acting, I always felt secure. I knew what I was doing. I had learned how to make myself look great and even to shine.

But I noticed that in my everyday life, there were too many situations in which I felt uncomfortable, awkward, and ugly. I, whom the New York drama critics had described as "witty and wonderful . . . with the smooth cool beauty of a Gainsborough."

Of course, I had thought it wasn't the "real me" they were reviewing. Surely, it was the character....

But it was also me, and only me, up there on those stages, feeling free enough to be and reveal those different, witty, wonderful parts of myself.

I got tired of feeling stupid and inadequate in life. I realized I could use the preparation and work that went into giving a dazzling performance on stage to make "real-life" situations that made me uncomfortable easier to handle, and even fun.

I made a list of some of the techniques that actors have used for hundreds of years, tools that have helped them to achieve the confidence and joy they need for any good performance. I realized that the same tools could help anyone achieve confidence and joy in their real life.

This book describes those techniques, how and why they work, and contains stories from famous actors and ordinary people, all of whom have used them successfully both on and off stage. Including me.

This book is not meant to teach you how to lie, but to help you find ways to be more authentically yourself. With all your humor, grace, and depth. With all your strength, uniqueness, and joy.

The first time I ever consciously used an acting technique in my "real life," I was frankly amazed that it actually worked. I found myself in a situation where I had to spend time with a man who it seemed could not be in the same room with me without mocking me, belittling me, or in some way putting me down. His put-downs made me want to shrivel up and die. The times I had to see him became unbearable.

Then, one day, I pretended that he had leprosy. I just told myself, "He has leprosy." I didn't imagine boils on his face, or bones sticking out of his hands, I just said, "I'll try it. I'll pretend he has leprosy."

I was using a simple acting technique called the Magic As If. I merely acted "as if" he had leprosy. It worked.

For one thing, it helped me to avoid him. After all, I was pretending he had some terrible disease that I could actually catch, why would I have wanted to get near him? So for starters, I never got close enough for him to start in.

Then, later that day, the guy actually told his wife, "Jane seemed better tonight, didn't you think?"

It's anybody's guess why he thought this. Did he feel compassion from me for his disease (his meanness)? Or was it that, because I avoided him, he was no longer threatened by my energy, and therefore didn't feel the need to try to diminish it or me. The point is, it worked, and I felt wonderful for a number of reasons. For one thing, I had a secret, and this made me feel good. Also, I was being creative. I was no longer a passive victim; I had become consciously active. An actor. And this made me feel good. And finally, he wasn't putting me down anymore. That made me feel wonderful.

Sometime after that, I began teaching acting techniques to other people, to help *them* in difficult real-life situations, job interviews, blind dates, family reunions, any situation that they wished could be easier. These people started using the techniques, and the situations became easier. Sometimes, they even became fun. This I liked. This *they* liked. The way I see it, if we have a choice between having a situation be difficult or fun, it might as well be fun.

I hope you will have fun reading this book, and that you, too, will change some of the more difficult situations in your life into experiences that you actually enjoy.

WHAT YOU'LL FIND IN THIS BOOK

THE ACTING TECHNIQUES described in this book are to help you through difficult real-life situations. If you are fantastically comfortable in any given situation, you probably don't need to use any of these techniques. Just close the book and go out and have a good time.

But if you've got a difficult situation, a difficult business meeting, presentation, blind date, or family reunion that's making you nervous, this book is for you. It's for those times when you're afraid you won't perform at your best, or that you'll lose your voice, get sweaty palms, start to shake, or even want to fall through the floor.

The job interviews, confrontations with your mother-in-law, special meetings, are all, in fact, potential performances, which might be as terrifying to you as the role of Hamlet might be to a nervous actor. I'm suggesting that what he would do to prepare for his performance might well be the same as what you might consider doing for yours.

Maybe you already know and use some of the techniques in this book. If so, I hope that reviewing them will suggest ways for you to make them even more powerful and effective. Some of the techniques may work better for you than others; some may not work for you at all. Some people get one technique quickly; others may need to practice it longer before they're able to use it. Keep experimenting.

All the techniques in the book are designed to help you to be all that you can be. As tall and as shining, and with as much charisma as you could ever want. Or as centered, clear, relaxed, self-confident, strong, or as witty as you want to be in any situation you choose. I learned these techniques from the forty teachers with whom I've studied over the last thirty years, as well as from other actors with whom I've worked. My students have shown me how everyone can use them and have taught me how to teach them to the layman.

Part One of this book describes a number of ways that actors prepare before going on stage or before a camera—many of which may be useful to you. You may not need to do all six parts of the preparation in Part One. Or you may want to come up with your own combination of exercises. But preparations can be essential because they can help you be however you decide you want to be, not only for a big presentation, but also for a big party—before which you might take a special shower, or dress in a particular way, or focus on why you're going. Maybe it's to find a new friend, or to recruit new clients. Maybe you simply have to program yourself to have a good time.

I include a chapter on your physical preparation—after all, your body plays an important role in how you feel and how you perceive yourself. The preparation is short but effective, and a big help for getting your body under control. There's also a chapter for your vocal preparation, so you can make your voice as strong, resonant, or as appropriate as you want. The emotional preparation is useful so you're not sabotaged by unexamined and unexpected feelings showing up—which could make you freeze, drop a glass, bump into a wall, or simply shake you up.

There's a preparation for revving up your brain, and one for getting your soul to shine through, since presumably, you'll also be bringing your mind and soul with you into that job interview or important meeting. The last preparation techniques are to help you to relax. Most actors understand that relaxation is essential for any good performance. When did you ever perform well when you were tense?

Part Two of the book includes eleven nuts-and-bolts techniques, how each technique works, and some scientific explanations of why. I'll show you how to understand, use, and practice each one. You'll read stories of people who have worked with me, how they use the specific technique, and how it helped them. There will be stories of actors who have used the same technique in a movie you may have seen. These techniques are easy and a lot of fun. I've found that the more fun they are, the more effectively they work for people.

In Part Three, I describe more tricks of the actor's trade, including how to have charisma, some vocal tricks, some breathing techniques and how to take a meaningful pause. Part Four offers more examples of difficult real-life situations—everything from finding a way to deliver a passionate sermon to learning to look and feel sexy, glamorous, or younger—and how non-actors working with me have been helped through them by using the techniques in this book.

Acting techniques, yoga, meditation, sex, or drugs can all change your brain chemistry. The choice is yours.

HOW TO USE THIS BOOK EFFECTIVELY

I SUGGEST YOU start at the beginning. The six-part preparation can be essential to opening yourself up enough to use the techniques I describe in Parts Two and Three.

On the other hand, if you feel that you're relaxed and open enough, it's possible you could turn to any one of the techniques in Part One and Two, get the technique in a flash, and immediately put it to work in your life. It's also true that the preparations include some very useful and powerful techniques.

Sense Memory, the first technique I describe in Part Two, is the basis for many of the techniques that follow, so I would advise reading about it before the others.

The last section of the book really should be read last since it describes how non-actors have made certain difficult real-life situations easy, or even fun, by using a combination of the techniques described in earlier chapters.

Not all of the techniques in this book will work for you, just as professional actors find that some techniques work for them and others don't. It all comes down to which techniques you are comfortable using. Some actors use what is known as "the Method," which is characterized by their ability to generate real feeling through creating the proper conditions. Other actors use a system known as "the English School," meaning they work from the outside in (starting with the coat they might wear for a role, or the kind of voice they'll use) to get into character. Both kinds of actors can be brilliant.

For the movie *Marathon Man*, Dustin Hoffman, considered by many to be a Method actor, stayed up all night before shooting a scene in which he was supposed to appear completely exhausted, to achieve as real and as total an exhaustion as he possibly could. Sir Lawrence Olivier, of the English School, who was acting with him in the scene, saw him as he arrived on the set, and asked him why he hadn't slept all night. Hoffman said it was so he could appear, and, in fact, *be,* truly exhausted in the scene. Sir Lawrence asked him why he didn't just try "acting."

Actually, I think this is a mean story, but it does illustrate my point. What works for one actor may not work for another. What works for you may not work for someone else.

WHAT I WISH FOR YOU

FOR ME, ACTING has been a sacred art, a healing art, an art of self-transformation. This book is about changing how we are. It's about me transforming myself from a well-brought-up Bryn Mawr graduate into the slightly ditzy, verbally limited pet shop owner in the *Rocky* movies. It's about Melvin, an accountant from New Jersey who came to me terrified of meeting women, changing himself into a social animal that now enjoys going out and dating.

This book is about changes you can make in yourself so that there can be changes in your life. Change, or creation, is hard work, and usually attributed to the gods. You are about to embark on that holy journey. It is a serious journey, and while most people tend to be afraid of the unknown, it is a journey I feel could not only be fun for you but also give you a sense of the divine and ecstatic mystery of creation—which is what I think the art of acting is all about.

It is with joy and humility that I share some of these mysteries with you. May your growing pains be minimal, and may your transformations be all that you wanted them to be when you picked up this book, and more.

· Prepare ·
Like an Actor

PART ONE

Every actor I know has devised a preparation ritual that is his alone, and which he performs before every performance.

If I'm performing one of my one-woman plays in front of twenty-four hundred people, as I did at Lincoln Center (in *Reminiscences of Mozart by His Sister*), I'll use a longer version of the six-part preparation described in Part One; I might take all day. If I'm going to a party where I want to look good, I might do a shorter version, maybe twenty minutes. Before certain auditions or job interviews, I may only have time for a three-minute version.

One of my favorite preparation rituals is a long, relaxing bath, ideally with mineral salts and candlelight. Baths work for me. I come out feeling reborn. Of course, it's rare that you will always have the time or opportunity to take a bath before an audition, a job interview, or a business lunch.

The bottom line here is that you need to find the preparation that works best for you.

When Shelley Winters worked on Broadway, she began preparing for her eight P.M. performances at three in the afternoon. Exercises, relaxations, even eating and napping were, for her, part of the preparation she felt she needed to go on stage and shine. You may not have five hours to prepare for your performance. You may not need five hours. Take whatever time you need. And have fun.

1

• Your Physical • Preparation

SO YOU WANT to be an actor. In your own life, that is. Or rather, you *are* an actor in your own life. And you have this body, the "actor's instrument," as actors say, this bag of bones and muscles and brain that doesn't always do what you want it to. It freezes, it gets nervous, scared, it shakes, it slumps, and your voice doesn't behave the way you want it to. How do you control it all?

First, you have to know what it is you are trying to control: Your body. What does it look like?

FOCUS ON HOW YOU STAND

- ❑ Find a mirror. Without looking in it, go and stand in front of it and don't think about how you are standing. Stand as you would ordinarily stand.
- ❑ Now look.
- ❑ Are your feet under your hips? Or are they closer together? If they are, exaggerate this by holding your legs and feet

tightly together. Feel how precarious your balance is. Feel how all your organs are squeezed together, certainly not how they would function best. Imagine that someone suddenly attacks you. Is this an easy position from which to escape? No. And you want to be the strongest warrior self you can be.

- ❑ If your feet are wider than your hips, exaggerate *this* position, just to feel what you're doing to yourself when your feet are wider than your hips. Now imagine that you want to make a quick getaway. Hard, isn't it? Your legs aren't under you.
- ❑ The first part of your getting your body to do what you want it to do is to come to know it, to know how it looks, and to feel how it stands, so you can consciously control it. You need to remember that your body takes orders from you; you are not its victim.

Position your feet directly under your hips. Feel what it's like to be centered, with your feet planted strongly on the ground, as if you were summoning strength from the earth itself. Like a tree.

Some people believe they can feel energized from the charge of the earth itself, and feel it flowing into their bodies from the earth's center, making them stronger and more grounded. Can you?

Disciples of certain Chinese martial arts even believe that the iron at the center of the earth can be consciously magnetized by the iron in our own blood to make us stronger. Can you?

- ❑ Now go back to the mirror.
- ❑ Are your hands at your sides? If not, you should be aware of the conscious or unconscious impression you are making on people on whom you may be trying to make a good impression.
- ❑ Are you holding your hands behind your back? If you are, the message people will get, if only subliminally, is that you are hiding something. Our primal selves understand this. That is why we first showed strangers our open hands—to show we were not carrying a knife.

- ❏ Are your hands clasped in front of your genitals? If they are, people will unconsciously wonder why you feel a need to protect them, the creative point of power in any body. Obviously, this is not the ideal message you want to communicate.
- ❏ Let your arms hang at your sides, hands open. This gives the message that you are self-confident, with nothing to fear and nothing to hide.

IT WORKS FOR ACTORS, IT CAN WORK FOR YOU

Your physical preparation will teach you that if you stand as if you were self-confident, your psyche will start to believe you are.

Studies from the Dana Alliance for Brain Initiatives show that your physical behavior influences your brain chemistry just as your brain can influence your physical behavior. In other words, the more you stand as if you were self-confident, the more your brain will be convinced that that you are.

This is not an easy position, just to stand there, your feet facing forward, your legs under your hips, your hands at your sides. Not doing anything. Not holding on to your hands as if they were holding some invisible Linus blanket. You're just there, ready to see and be seen, to run or to fight. You'll look like a mountain of strength.

An actor gets on stage with her body, just as you walk into that boardroom or cocktail party with yours. That's all we've got that shows. We'd better get it into the best shape we can.

So, exercise. Most actors do. Diane Keaton goes to a gym. Sylvester Stallone lifts weights. Helen Hunt practices yoga. Get yourself into shape. Do anything that makes you and your body feel more alive. The more in touch you are with your body, the happier it will be, and the happier *you* will be. A happy body carries a happy person, and that's who you want to walk into a room.

Walk into that room *with* your body. Feeling it. Owning it. Walk in with as much of yourself as you can, and be as fully present as you can be. That's what we all want, not only from the actors we see, but also from the people we want to be around, and from ourselves: the fullest presence possible.

Spencer Tracy and Katharine Hepburn—they had enormous presences. You can as well, by not leaving your body behind when you present yourself to the world.

THE SUNKEN CHEST SYNDROME

SOME OF THE people who come to my workshops seem to have sunken chests. They look as if they were trying to squeeze their hearts back into their spines, as if that could stop their hearts from being broken—again. But let's face it, these people look awful. They want love, but they're walking into rooms with these depressed, sunken chests.

- ❑ Get back in front of that mirror.
- ❑ Do *you* have a sunken chest?
- ❑ If you do, try and imagine a balloon in that chest and blow it up. Feel it expand with magic helium. Any color you want. Not too much. Just until you look "normal."
- ❑ Images, like the balloon, will activate the right side of your brain, and speak directly to your unconscious. Our bodies often respond more quickly to images than to verbal commands, which speak to the left side of our brains.
- ❑ So there are many ways of expanding your chest. Even ways that are fun. For example, you might pretend you're your favorite medieval knight about to joust and feel the huge, heavy armor surrounding your chest, protecting your heart. Allow it to expand, let it take up as much space as you want.

SLUMPING SHOULDERS

HAVING YOUR SHOULDERS slumped forward is another way to protect your heart. Not that these postures do not have their place. They're great for groveling; but not if you want to walk into a room and impress everyone with your power, strength, and courage. Mainly, you want to impress *yourself* with your power, strength, and courage. And shoulders slumping forward just won't do it. If your body is in a depressed position, that's how you'll feel, and how you'll believe you are.

So, back in front of that mirror. Observe your shoulders: are they slumped forward? If so, move them back. You could do this by simply moving them back, or you might try using some imagery:

- ❏ You could imagine you're wearing a knapsack that automatically pulls your shoulders back. Put whatever you want in that knapsack. Maybe it's your favorite picnic lunch with your favorite dessert. Maybe it's a blanket for the grass where you're going to meet your lover, if that turns you on. Maybe you even have some sweet-smelling massage oil in there.
- ❏ Put six puppies in that sack if *that'll* turn you on. The goal in all of this is to be turned on. To feel alive. Put anything you want in that sack, just as long as you feel it pulling your shoulders down and away from your heart, so your heart is open now, free to feel love and be loved. Plus, you'll look like a person people will want to be around. Even a person *you'd* like to be around. Probably more than when your shoulders were slumped forward.
- ❏ Imaginary knapsacks work for some people and not for others. Maybe all you need is to tell yourself to bring your shoulders down and back. What helps some people is telling their shoulders to be over their hips. As if their shoulders and hips were having a conversation. And liked each other. And were in balance.

IT WORKS FOR ACTORS, IT CAN WORK FOR YOU

Balance is of course what all these exercises are about. Putting yourself in balance will help you feel centered when you walk into a room and confident that nothing will throw you *off* balance.

Dr. Stephen Stiteler, who specializes in oriental medicine and homeopathy in Los Angeles, reminded me that if your body is slumped, this posture will chemically affect how you feel and you will actually feel depressed. How could you not be depressed? Your organs will have less room to perform as they were meant to perform, and that is depressing.

STICKING YOUR NECK OUT

USE THAT MIRROR, or find a person to tell you how you look. Is your neck sticking out? If it is, you might notice how unattractive that looks. Worse, if your neck is pushed forward, you will notice that your hips are pulled back to balance the forward thrust of your head. No way can you move forward from this position as quickly as you might need, if, in fact, you needed to move quickly. Say, to escape an attacking lion.

Okay, there is probably no attacking lion, but when we are afraid, our bodies act *as if* there were a lion there. That's what stage fright is: the body acting, or rather reacting, as if its life were in danger. And our adrenaline starts flowing, and our muscles tighten and our throats dry up. But there is no lion.

I only bring up the lion because your body needs to know it could escape from danger if it needed to. You're in training to be your best warrior self, remember, and the more balanced your body is, the more able it is to fight or run away.

IT WORKS FOR ACTORS, IT CAN WORK FOR YOU

The exercises in this book are designed not only to let your body know it could escape a dangerous situation if you had to, but also to get your body to be as strong, as alive, and as balanced as possible.

THE ACTOR'S PHYSICAL WARM-UP: YOUR NECK

WHAT'S IMPORTANT IN the physical warm-up is to get to know your body, so you can have some control over it, just the way you wish you had control over those occasional sweaty palms or a voice that is suddenly an octave higher than you wish it were.

Your neck connects your body with your brain. We want the communication between your body and your brain to be as effective as it can possibly be. Plus, according to some, the neck is considered the creative and communicative center of the body. So of course you want to get to know it, relax it, and control it.

If your neck is tense, your vocal cords are constricted and the sounds you make will be pretty unattractive. Try lifting your shoulders to strangle your neck and try speaking. Not a lovely sound, is it? A relaxed neck is essential for optimal vocal production.

If you are already exercising, doing marathons, or are a ballet dancer or swimmer, you may already have the physical awareness of your neck that is essential for optimum communication and self-presentation.

Here are the exercises I give people in my workshops:

- ❑ Slowly drop your head straight down so it hangs off your neck.
- ❑ Slowly raise your head, vertebra by vertebra, until you can once again look straight ahead of yourself. As you raise your

head, imagine yourself breathing shining white light into the spaces between the vertebrae. (See chapter 19 on Breathing, to understand how and why these conscious breaths are so useful. For one thing, you will be helping oxygen to get into your brain so you can think more clearly.)

- ❏ Slowly lift your head back so you're arching your neck and your eyes are on the ceiling. Be careful not to compress the back of your neck.
- ❏ Slowly bring your head back to center, so you are once again looking straight ahead of yourself, again breathing shining white light into the spaces between the vertebrae.
- ❏ Repeat the above steps. In other words, drop your chin to your chest, and then bring it back to center, breathing shining light (for charisma) into the spaces between your vertebrae. Then drop it back, and bring it back to center.
- ❏ Now turn your head all the way to your left, breathing white light into the upward spiral you are seeming to create out of your neck. Just trust me about the white light. Scientific studies show that light has strengthening and healing properties. If you read chapter 7 on Sense Memory, you will understand why real light beamed into the spaces between your vertebrae will have the same effect on your body as imaginary light.
- ❏ Bring your head back to center, still imagining it is spiraling upward.
- ❏ Swivel your neck slowly to the right, breathing into your spiraling neck. Bring your head back to center.
- ❏ Repeat the spirals to the left and to the right.
- ❏ Now drop your left ear toward your left shoulder, consciously pulling down the right shoulder. Breathe into the curve of your neck as if it were a rainbow. The rainbow is optional, although I'm always impressed by the studies showing how right-brain pictorial images are often more effective at getting our bodies to change than linear, left-brain commands.
- ❏ Bring your head back to center.

- ❑ Drop your right ear toward your right shoulder and stretch the neck as described above.
- ❑ Bring your head back to center.

A BONUS FOR YOUR NECK

I PARTICULARLY LOVE the following exercise for a number of reasons. It is a moment for you to be good and loving to yourself, a time for your body to hear that somebody cares if it's in pain and will take care of it. This is the antidote to stage fright in life. Usually, the fear that most of us experience, that stops us from being all that we can be, is an unconsciously initiated *physical* reaction to something that our adult, rational mind knows is not scary at all.

- ❑ Drop your left ear to your left shoulder. Now use either hand to massage the right side of your neck.
- ❑ Look for any tense muscles. Is your trapezius masquerading as a bone? (Your trapezius is the muscle that goes from your neck down and out to your shoulders.)
- ❑ Use your fingers to massage away any tension in the muscles that go from your head to your shoulder, allowing new space in between the tight muscles, tendons, and tissue.

If, for example, when we were five years old, some eager friend of our mother happened to grab our cute little cheeks in her powerful hands, to tell us how cute we were, pinching us, possibly even leaving a red mark, years later if we should meet someone wearing the perfume the pincher had worn, we will get tense and uncomfortable—even though we might not understand our reaction. It is a memory in our bodies from our past that causes our present discomfort. It is our silenced five-year-old screaming "Get your big fat thumbs off my face!" Or something like that.

What we really need at that moment for our child/body/unconscious child is a grown-up voice telling us: "I care. Everything will be all right. You will be taken care of." And that, in essence, is the message that your hand is communicating to your neck as you are evening out those tense spots, saying in effect, "I love you. I don't want you to have pain. I want you to feel good and be all that you are and can be." When we feel unloved, unsafe, and bad about ourselves, we rarely perform at our best.

So back to that bonus for your neck:

- ❑ Drop your right ear to your right shoulder. Massage the muscles and tendons of the left side of your neck with either hand.
- ❑ Is this side more or less tense than the other?
- ❑ Do you feel you deserve to be treated this well? It is always interesting to me to notice which people in my workshops stop this pleasurable exercise before I suggest they finish. Some people do have trouble being nice to themselves, which is unfortunately a stumbling block to their feeling joy in their lives, not to mention in their self-presentation.
- ❑ Now bring your head back to center.
- ❑ How does your neck feel? Different than when you started this very simple warm-up? You bet.

WARMING UP YOUR SPINE

SOMETIMES I MEASURE the height of the people who take my workshops when they walk in the door, and very often, after they leave, they actually measure one half inch taller than when they walked into the room. And since you know what you want is to be all you can be, you might as well be as tall as you can be.

The following exercise essentially gives your body permission not to shrink, which it does when it is afraid, but instead to be as large, as tall, and as magnificent as possible.

- ❑ Standing straight, feet parallel, drop your chin slowly to your chest. Allow your head to fold toward the floor, bending over at the hips. I suggest you leave your knees bent, so there's no danger of you hurting your back.
- ❑ Make sure your neck is loose. You can test this by moving your head back and forth and around to make sure you are not holding any tension in your neck.
- ❑ Slowly come back to standing position, stacking your vertebrae one at a time, consciously breathing white light into the spaces between the vertebrae.
- ❑ Do it again. It should feel great. After all, when you are hanging upside down, your body is basically in traction. So you are doing some very good things for yourself. You are forcing blood into your brain without it having to work so hard against gravity. Plus, since you are upside down, gravity is not pressing your vertebrae down on the disks of your spine. Those disks need their space!

WARMING UP YOUR ARMS AND LEGS

THE FOLLOWING EXERCISE I learned in a yoga class. Its results are quick and thrilling to me. See what you think.

- ❑ Hold your right arm in front of you, shoulder height, with your elbow bent, and begin to try to shake your right hand off of your arm, moving your loose hand from left to right very, very, very fast.
- ❑ Now hold your right arm out straight in front of you, as stiffly and as rigidly as you can, fingers extended, as far apart as possible, tight, tight, tight.
- ❑ Drop your arm to your side.
- ❑ Notice how it feels. Tingling and alive?
- ❑ And how does the other arm feel? Dead? Probably.
- ❑ Repeat the above exercise with your left hand and arm:

shaking, extending, and then feeling their aliveness. You may even notice the left arm now feels more alive than the right. Oh well.

- ❑ Now, stand on your left leg. You may want to use a wall or chair to help you balance. Try to shake your right leg out of its hip socket, and your right foot off of its ankle.
- ❑ Keep shaking that leg, imagining extra space in your hip socket, knee, and ankle.
- ❑ Now put your right foot back on the floor.
- ❑ Compare your right leg to your left. The right feels more alive and aware, doesn't it? You might as well do the left leg and get a little balance in your life.

I love this exercise because in practically no time at all I get to feel what it feels like to have one arm so alive and the other so seemingly unconscious. And when you go into that boardroom or to lunch with that bank president, you want to feel and appear as alive as possible. It's the people who are truly alive that most people want to work with. No one wants to work with someone who is dead.

I figure if I have a choice in this short life, of being alive and conscious or being asleep, I want to choose alive and conscious—however difficult that choice may sometimes be.

Now you have warmed up your physical body. How does it feel? More alive? Could the two of you be having a better relationship with each other than when you started these exercises? I hope so, because we want to have the most control over our bodies that we can.

2

• Your Vocal • Preparation

A LOT OF people come to me who don't like how their voices sound, usually, because they think their voices are too thin, or too quiet. Sometimes they're right. They want to impress a blind date or a prospective client, but their voices are much thinner than they wish they were, and in fact much thinner they were meant to be. Most people use only a fraction of their vocal power; much the way people use only a small percentage of their brainpower.

In many ways, our society is set up so that people end up speaking less resonantly than they were built to speak. Parents, like our society, are always telling us to be quiet and not to make too many waves, which, we are taught, can be dangerous. We don't need McCarthy or the National Endowment of the Arts to tell us that free speech can be hazardous to our health.

Of course, if everyone were running around freely expressing himself, in every and any way that might come into his head, yes, there might be chaos. But that's hardly the problem here.

One of the most exciting aspects for me about teaching vocal exercises is that I get to introduce people to the fun and joy of using their full voices. I confess, I too sometimes forget how much fun it is to use my voice. To feel the words in my mouth. To feel them explode through my lips and reverberate in my head.

Our whole body, in fact, has an amazing capacity to vibrate with sound, as if it were some miraculous violin. Of course, it's not a violin; but our faces, our cheekbones, our heads, chest cavity, and our bones vibrate no less extraordinarily, fully, and resonantly than the brilliantly calibrated body of a Stradivarius.

People still think of the quiet child as the Good Child. Well-behaved children are quiet. Good children are "seen and not heard." Many of us learn to be quiet to survive our childhood, and many of us need to re-educate ourselves in order to speak out with our true voices.

The actor Ron Liebman, who won a Tony Award for his astounding performance as Roy Cohn in the Broadway production of *Angels in America,* does vocal warm-ups every night before going on stage. So did Sir Lawrence Olivier.

The trick to releasing your voice is, I believe, to find those exercises that not only allow your voice to free itself, but are also easy and fun. Here are two exercises I give in my workshops, which usually get immediate and even amazing results.

THE LOUD "HAAAH"

- ❑ Stand with your feet directly under your hips.
- ❑ Open your mouth as wide as you can.
- ❑ Push your middle fingers into the hinges of your jaw. Really open up that space. Allow your fingers to massage the line that goes from the mandibular joint down to the corners of your mouth. Are you tense there? Most people are. If you are, massage those tense muscles.
- ❑ Why have I asked you to open your mouth so wide? Because it's good to have an open and relaxed mouth when you speak. To let out the words. It's hard to make a round and resonant

sound if your mouth is closed. Try to talk with your mouth closed. Not a pleasant sound, is it. So, just for this exercise, open your mouth as wide as you can. Not that you will eventually be walking around with your mouth hanging open, as if you were going to catch a tennis ball. Open your mouth wide so that your muscles can experience what it's like to feel more open than they probably are used to being. So you can roar. Not that you have to go around roaring, but it's important that you begin to experience the range of your voice and the limits of its power.

- ❑ Check in a mirror or with someone else, to make sure that your chin is not jutting forward or back when you are opening your mouth wide. Check that your eyes are looking straight ahead of you.
- ❑ Now, put one of your hands on your chest. Tap your chest with your hand as if it were a drum that will vibrate with sound. You will do this when you make the sound, both to make sure that your chest is vibrating, and to remind yourself that your voice comes not from your throat but from deeper and further down in your body. Some actors imagine they are speaking from their genitals, but let's start with the chest.
- ❑ Take in a deep breath. Feel your lungs expand behind you, as well as in your chest and at your sides. I know what a revelation it was to me when I first understood that my back could expand with my breathing.

I had forgotten that I had a back. As if I had forgotten that I had a history. Until then, I had imagined myself walking into a room only putting my best face forward. And so I had diminished my entrance.

IT WORKS FOR ACTORS, IT CAN WORK FOR YOU

Be multidimensional when you walk into a room, not only with a front but also with a back and sides, so you make an entrance with your whole self. If you want to make an impressive entrance, you've got to bring as much of you in there as possible.

- ❑ Take another deep breath and make sure your belly expands with air. This is not the time for false vanity. If you want a strong and resonant voice, it must be supported by expanding your belly. Sorry. (Try speaking without your belly full of air and hear how much thinner your voice sounds than when it's full.)
- ❑ Now let out a loud "Haaah" sound on that deep breath you just took (front, back, sides). Don't forget that first "H." It will connect your sound to your diaphragm, so that the sound is supported by your body and you don't try to make the sound with just your throat muscles. A sound manufactured in your throat will not only be thin and unattractive, but also, if practiced consistently, could give you nodes on your vocal chords. Not good.
- ❑ Repeat that "Haaah" sound. Your mouth is wide open and your hand is tapping on your chest, feeling it vibrate with the sound. Force yourself to make as loud a "Haaah" as possible. You might imagine you are calling to someone across the street or down the block, someone you really hope will hear you. Like the man with an enormous inheritance check for you from a relative you never knew existed.

DARING TO HAVE A FULL AND POWERFUL VOICE

HAVE YOU EVER been at a play and suddenly an actor came on stage and you couldn't take your eyes off him? You may recall that he had an extremely rich and resonant voice. What actually happened is that his chest bone was vibrating with sound and it set up a corresponding vibration in your own chest. And you're hooked; you're vibrating together. This is a neat trick when you want anyone or even everyone to pay attention to you. The Haaah exercise allows you to focus on your chest bones vibrating with sound.

Some of my clients are scared by the power of their own voices. Some of them have never made as loud a sound as they make with me. Their lives have never required that they be loud. They've managed to miss ball games and bullfights. Maybe they're from a culture that frowns on anything but quiet, hushed tones. But then they start making loud sounds with me, in spite of being scared, and they manage to survive.

Do the Haaah exercise a few times and see how it feels. At first, you may be surprised or even nervous. Eventually, it should only feel terrific.

I once spent a weekend up at Muhammad Ali's training camp. (I wasn't training to be a boxer, my boyfriend at the time was taking photos of him for a magazine.) Ali was at his fighting best and I will never forget him, early in the morning, flinging open the door of his trailer, pounding on his chest, and booming out into the hills, "I'M THE GREATEST!"

Somehow he instinctively knew this booming voice would tell the rest of his body that he was strong and victorious. And for a while, he was.

Hearing the force of our loudest roars, feeling our bodies vibrate with a deep booming sound, forces us to acknowledge our power. Go for it.

THE UPSIDE-DOWN "HAAAH"

THIS EXERCISE WILL show your body what it feels like to have a loose neck. A tight one will constrict your vocal production and the sounds you produce will sound thin, tinny, and strangled. Try lifting your shoulders up to your ears to tighten your neck, and try to speak. An unpleasant sound, isn't it? So here's the exercise:

- ❏ With your feet under your hips, allow your head to drop down until it's in front of your knees, so that your spine is hanging upside down from your hips. You are folded over, as you were in the warm-up for the spine. Remember to bend your knees a little to avoid any back injury.
- ❏ Now take in a deep breath. Upside down. Notice how easy it is to feel your lungs expand in your back. Amazing, isn't it?
- ❏ Make sure your neck is loose. Allow your head to nod up and down and even make circles to make sure.
- ❏ Make the Haaah sound from this upside-down position, making sure your neck keeps loose.
- ❏ Try to memorize how your neck feels. With your head shaking around, not to mention its weight pulling your neck into traction, it's pretty hard to have any neck tension. That's what you want to feel, because it's neck tension that constricts your voice and makes it less than it can be.
- ❏ Now stand up, but slowly, because you should have a substantial amount of blood in your head and we don't want you to pass out. Even after you are standing straight again, keep your eyes on the floor. Then lift them to eye level.
- ❏ Now try to make the Haaah sound and see if you can feel the same looseness in your neck that you felt when you were upside down. If you feel tension creeping back, you could either flop upside down again to remember what it's like to be without neck tension, or, standing up, you could wriggle your neck around so that it doesn't get stuck in a petrified

position. You can also try wriggling your whole body around to loosen it up, so that there is no muscular tension anywhere to block the sound from releasing.

Go ahead, feel like a fool. Make an ass of yourself. Feel silly. Be silly. Many of my students start to feel silly and embarrassed here. I say, "Silliness is next to godliness."

THE HMMMM

YOUR FACE, YOUR nose, your teeth, your entire skull can resonate like a drum. Here's an exercise that will encourage them do that, so you can feel them resonating:

- ❑ Take in a deep breath.
- ❑ Make a loud "H" sound (Huh).
- ❑ Keep your lips pressed together and add a humming "MMMMM" sound to the "Huh." "HUMMMMM."
- ❑ Repeat it. "HUMMMMM." Try to make the sound as loud as you can. Again, you might try to have someone across the street hear you. And feel your lips vibrating a lot. As if you were playing with tissue paper on a comb.

I love this exercise for two reasons. First, because the "H" activates the diaphragm, so the sound starts in your solar plexus and not in your throat, and there's no way it can be tight. Second, because you really cannot tighten your throat when you make this sound and a tight throat is the enemy of free, resonant vocal production. "Hmmmm." Feel that vibrating? Doesn't that feel good?

Make this "Hmmmm" sound for as long as one breath lasts you. Then do it again. Six, seven, or eight times if you're up to it.

SAYING YOUR NAME OUT LOUD

After doing the "Hmmmm" and the two "Haaah" exercises, say your name out loud. Most people are shocked to hear their voices sound so much deeper and more resonant than before they did these two little, seemingly simple exercises. Can *you* hear the change?

To make sure you have gotten all the benefits you can from these two first exercises:

- ❑ Keep your hand on your chest to make sure it is vibrating with sound.
- ❑ Start with "Hmmmm."
- ❑ Go into "My name is ______." So it should sound like "Hummmm-mmmmy-name is ______."

The "Hmmmm" gets the sound vibrating in your teeth and mouth cavity. Let it push right into the "M" of *my,* and try and keep the sound behind your teeth, so you're not swallowing the sound out of some unconscious fear that someone will hear you.

Can you hear how different your voice sounds from before you did the exercises? If not, you might want to record your voice before and after you do them. Some people are scared of the new voice they hear. They think it is too loud, too powerful, too strong. They fear that it will alienate people. Probably the way they alienated their parents when they were young and made more noise than was comfortable for their parents. Probably the way their parents had alienated their own parents when they were young.

If you are one of these people, recording your voice might be helpful for you to realize that your new, strong voice is not as booming and terrible as you might have feared. Our goal here is to eliminate our parents' fears and to own the strong and wonderful voices we were all given.

Be all you can be vocally. It's hard not to be impressed by someone with vocal presence.

IT WORKS FOR ACTORS, IT CAN WORK FOR YOU

A strong vocal presence commands attention and respect—which you deserve to get.

So do these exercises. Anywhere. In the shower, in your car, or on your way to a presentation. And I hope you really start to enjoy your new voice.

MICHAEL LOOSENS UP

MICHAEL, A THIRTY-FOUR-YEAR-OLD accountant, came to me because he knew he was going to have to give some business presentations, and he was scared. He was quiet and shy, and not comfortable talking with most people.

When he spoke, I could hear how his voice was stuck somewhere in the back of his throat. He was actually a tall and powerful-looking man, but he had the voice of a much smaller man. In fact, he had the voice of a much smaller man who was practically whispering. His voice was muffled and stifled in the back of his throat, and not making it forward to benefit from all the resonance of his head and face.

So I said, "Put the sound forward, don't leave it back." When I said, "Put the sound forward," I made a rich, round sound as I illustrated a full, forward-placed speaking voice that bounced off my teeth, like the sounds you felt in the "Hmmmm" exercise. When I said, "Don't leave it back," I forced my voice to slide back down my throat, squelched and half-swallowed.

I asked him to try to imitate what I had done. I asked him to feel the words "Put the sound forward" exploding out of his teeth, resonating in his head, and to feel the words "Don't leave it back," tight and strangled in the back of his throat.

He was hesitant and slow to catch on. So I took him through it a word at a time. Until we were having fun.

We started with the "P" in put. I asked him to say, "Puh. Puh. Puh."

I asked him to say it louder. Explosively. A drum on his lips. A sensual experience. Until he started to enjoy making the sound.

He was not used to enjoying making sounds. He was used to feeling afraid of making too much noise. For which, I'd like to thank Michael's parents, and parents everywhere who in some way or other punish their children for making too much noise, or sometimes any noise at all, and are at the root of this vocal problem.

Then we got to the "t" in "put." I asked him to say, "Tuh. Tuh. Tuh." He said, "Tuh. Tuh. Tuh."

I pushed him to make the sound louder, the "t" more explosive against the front of the roof of his mouth. He almost began to enjoy himself.

When we got to the word "sound," we had a field day. First, we hissed the initial "s." Like gas escaping, or a snake hissing. "Ssssss."

When we got to the vowel sound in "sound," I tried to get him to be more outrageous than Eliza Doolittle. "Aaaooow." I had us both opening our mouths as wide as we could to make the roundest, fullest sounds we could.

I wouldn't let him miss the potential joy of sounding the "n" in the word. I had him draw out the sound as if he were playing the most romantic violin imaginable. "Nnnnnn." I had him do it until he felt the roof of his mouth vibrating, till he felt his whole head vibrating. "Nnnnnn."

Then we started putting the sounds together. "SSSSSAAA-OOOWWNNNNN."

And then we added the final, explosive "D." "SSSSSAAA-OOOWWNNNNND."

We repeated it over and over again. At first he was scared. He was not used to having so much sound come out of his mouth or to feeling so many vibrations in his head. But it got to be fun. He began to feel his power, and to realize that it was safe to feel his power.

THE OUTRAGEOUS SOUND AND DANCE EXERCISE

THEN I ASKED Michael to join me dancing around as we said the words. Well, not formally dancing, but moving around, as freely as we could. So our bodies were loose, even silly, so that the words wouldn't get trapped anywhere, so that the expression of the sound wouldn't be blocked anywhere in the body. Not in the throat, or in the shoulders, or in the pelvis.

He felt embarrassed, silly.

I asked him to try to enjoy feeling silly.

I said, "Go on, make a fool out of yourself. No one's looking but me, and let's face it, I'm making an even bigger fool of myself than you are, and you haven't walked out yet. As a matter of fact, not only are you not walking out, you're even paying me to carry on like this."

Then I had us begin to make stupid faces as we spoke the words. "Put the sound forward, don't leave it back." By the time we had finished, the lines in his face had begun to relax, and he looked five years younger.

Michael had a tendency to want to rush the words, as if he didn't feel he deserved to take up time. As if his hurrying would make him less visible and less likely to be punished for being heard. I asked him to say the words as slowly and as stupidly as he could, as if he were an idiot. This made him laugh. And even this was good for him. For one thing, his having fun was strengthening his ability to feel good.

Plus the laughter was actually strengthening his immune system. Studies at the Norman Cousins Center for Psycho-neuroimmunology at UCLA have shown that when we laugh, our bodies produce a chemical that actually strengthens our immune systems!

Michael was beginning to feel good, and to feel safe. Which is how he wants to feel when he gives those presentations. But he wasn't used to feeling good or feeling safe. He needed to practice. And somehow, by having fun doing this exercise, he started feeling safe and good. He even started feeling loved and cared for, as if somebody were giving him a good time. And someone was. It was himself. And he began to feel he deserved it.

That's the state we all want to be in when we give those dreaded presentations. Frankly, I think it'd be lovely if we were all feeling this way all of the time. But for now, we're just making sounds.

MAKING SOUNDS IS GOOD FOR YOU

AT FIRST, MICHAEL had felt uncomfortable simply making sounds that on their own didn't seem to make any sense. So I talked about the healing properties of sound. I mentioned the pure sounds of the yoga mantras, sounds that for thousands of years have healed troubled bodies and spirits that are out of balance.

I talked about the ancient yoga practice of chanting "Om," a sound that is said to vibrate with everything in the universe that is in harmony with it or, as some people believe, which vibrates with the primal creative energy of the universe. Perhaps that is why repeating "Om" has been shown to balance our nervous systems.

Sound after all is a powerful energy, which, like so many of the tools in this book, if used correctly, can be transformative. Scientific studies show plants grow either more quickly or more slowly, depending on what kind of music they are played. Johann Sebastian Bach apparently makes them flourish. Rock and roll makes it harder for them to grow. (I hope this is different for humans.) Sound, after all, is only vibrations at different frequencies.

Sound is also used by sports doctors today, with machines that transmit ultrasound waves into injured muscles and tendons to speed up their healing.

At first, Michael had felt uncomfortable doing the Outrageous Sound and Dance Exercise. He was not used to waving his arms around, shaking his hips, and letting his tongue fall out of his mouth. I reassured him that this was not how he was being trained to act in public.

On a shyness scale of a hundred and eighty degrees, Michael's shyness was initially at a hundred and eighty, his feeling at ease in public, at zero. He needed to be at ninety. We had a better chance of getting him there if we went for broke, if he learned how to be totally outrageous, if his body and spirit and feelings experienced the limit of their exhibitionism. I knew that if he discovered how far, in fact, he could go, he would be able to find a middle ground.

And he did. At least, his voice is a lot stronger and more resonant than when he started working with me. People pay attention when he shows up to give a presentation. And best of all, he doesn't hate his voice anymore. And he shouldn't.

I think everyone should like his own voice. Do you like yours?

3

Your Emotional Preparation

I FIND EMOTIONAL preparation as important, if not sometimes more important, than any other kind of preparation. Sometimes this is all I need to get myself centered, in touch, and fully present, so I can walk into any difficult situation and feel and behave as I want.

Maybe you've experienced how easy it is to muck things up if you go somewhere and you don't know how you feel.

AN UNFORTUNATE AUDITION

I ONCE HAD an audition in California before I started teaching acting techniques for everyday life. It was for a very important casting director, one who had either seen or knew about the one-woman show I'd done several years earlier in New York, to rave reviews. She'd had me in for an audition then, but she hadn't called me back to audition since. Not once. And this made me angry. Didn't she know how brilliant I was? How dare she! Wasn't I good enough? What did she think I was, chopped liver?

I was angry. But I didn't know I was angry. I'd been trained to think and believe and behave as if everything was always "fine." After all, good little girls didn't get angry, and only good little girls had a chance of surviving where I grew up. So I was just about the sweetest, most polite, most well behaved little young lady you could ever have wished to see. (All of which sounds pretty disgusting to me now. No wonder she hadn't called me in.)

The point is, I was angry, but I didn't know it. I barely knew what "angry" was. And I certainly wouldn't have known what to do with the anger if I *had* known. So I walked into that audition thinking everything was fine, and I looked down at the scene I'd prepared to read, and I read.

It was a simple scene and I thought I'd be brilliant, as I knew I could be. But I wasn't. I was awful. I could hardly see the page I was holding, no less read it because of my unconscious anger. I could barely keep my body still and doing what I wanted it to be doing. Like focusing on the script. Because I had all this anger charging around in me and blocking the flow of any real creativity, not to mention my reading skills.

What I really wanted to do was to yell, "HOW THE HELL COULD YOU NOT HAVE CALLED ME IN FOR ALL THESE YEARS, YOU STUPID, POCK-MARKED POWER MONGER OF A BLEEP, BLEEP, BLEEP. . . ."

But I didn't know I wanted to swear at her. (Yeah, *that* would have helped me get the job.) In fact, I was so busy keeping my anger unconscious, that I was, in fact, at war with myself, with one part of me angry and another part working hard to make sure I didn't know it. Of course I made a mess of the audition. The words could barely come out right.

If I'd *known* how I felt, I would at least not have been my own enemy. I could have analyzed the painful feelings underneath the anger. Or maybe, had I been *conscious* of the anger, I could have "used it," as we actors say, to fill the scene with its energy, pretending it was the character's anger and energy. At least I would have been *conscious,* and I would have had a chance of being as brilliant as I'd wanted to be. I wouldn't have used up all my energy trying not to feel how I was feeling.

And now? What would I do now, if I had to audition for someone who, let's say, had refused to see me for a number of years?

Well, first, before I went in, I'd really check in with how I was feeling. Probably angry. And then, underneath, probably hurt.

And then I'd let myself feel and say to myself whatever I was thinking. Maybe, "Doesn't she think I'm any good? Don't *I* think I'm any good? Do I feel worthless because she isn't validating me? When, in my childhood, did I feel worthless because I wasn't validated? Is my little girl reliving some old fear from when some parent made her feel worthless, so she thought her life was in danger because that parent was angry?"

In other words, now I'd feel my feelings. The fear. The pain. All of it. And I'd tell that childhood self, "You're safe, now, and I'll take care of you. Because I love you a lot, and I think you're wonderful. So there." That usually gets rid of my fear and pain.

Also, now, I might be able to let go of my anger by forgiving the casting person for not having called me in, by trying to understand her side of it. Maybe I had reminded her of her mother and she hates her mother. Maybe she had been allergic to the perfume I'd been wearing that day, so many years ago. Maybe her boyfriend had just left her. When I can forgive her, and myself for being angry with her, there's a good chance my anger won't block my creativity. So I can just walk into that audition room and do a great reading.

Have *you* ever gone somewhere, sure you'd handle a situation well, and then, out of some unconscious feeling, suddenly, as if by accident, you knock over a lamp or drop a glass? That's what the Emotional Preparation is designed to prevent. So you find out how you're feeling before you walk into the situation, not after it's too late.

GETTING IN TOUCH WITH YOUR FEELINGS

How in touch are you?

- **For example, are you afraid about that speech you're going to give?**
- **Or excited?**
- **Did you know that fear and excitement photograph as the same energy when photographed with a Kirolean camera, which can take pictures of energy fields? The fear is a pattern based on past terrors, the excitement, on future hopes.**
- **And what about that blind date? Are you afraid? Excited? Isn't it a relief to realize you may be both afraid *and* excited, and not just afraid?**

Are you excited to be going out with that Nobel Prize winner, or are you blocking your fear, and thinking everything is "fine," so that when he shows up, you can't talk?

How you feel and how you figure it out is what the Emotional Preparation is all about.

FEELINGS IN THE BODY

I MAKE THE Emotional Preparation a two-part process, so I have twice as good a chance of not missing anything. I'm trying to get in touch with my feelings, and I start with the body, which is where all the feelings are hiding.

Try this exercise sitting in a chair. Keep your feet apart, and don't let your hands touch. One hand on each knee, palms up, is usually good. In this position you're more open to your feelings, and the feelings can flow through you most easily. So you can feel them more easily, which, let's face it, is what the exercise is all about.

You can also try the exercise lying down. Maybe lying down is better for you than sitting up. Find out.

Close your eyes and ask yourself how you're feeling—in your body. Is there a muscle that's tight, or tense, or in other words, in pain? For me, physical pain is always a mirror of some emotional pain. And I don't need that pain if I'm going to be brilliant on that stage or in that room. The pain just clogs up my energy flow and distracts me from being as brilliant as I can be.

So, your eyes are closed and you're asking yourself, "How is my body feeling? Is there any pain or tension?" Really try and locate the tension. We're not all that used to allowing ourselves to acknowledge our pain. "Stiff upper lip" and all that. The "I'm fine" syndrome. Maybe you, too, were taught, "No one will love you if you cry or complain." You won't be the first person who was programmed to think that.

Let's say you've located a pain. Maybe in your back, on the left side. That's the first step. Locating it and acknowledging it. Now see if you can figure out what it's about. Did something happen today that you haven't acknowledged? Did someone hurt your feelings and you haven't wanted to admit it?

If you can't think of a reason for the pain, so you can't just cry about, say, losing your job ("I lost my job, I'll miss the people there, I feel like a loser") just try and locate the pain physically. *Where* does it hurt? Where *exactly*?

- ❑ Can you give an image to the pain?
- ❑ Can you give it a shape and a color? Let's say you can, and you see the pain as red and shaped like a lima bean—about two and a half inches by four and a half inches. The more specific you can be, the easier it will be to get rid of it. You have to see the enemy before you can blow him away.
- ❑ Now imagine you are breathing white light into the red lima bean. Breathe deep.
- ❑ Keep seeing the lima bean; keep seeing the white light flood into it.

- ❑ Repeat five times.
- ❑ Now, focus on the lima bean. What do you see? The red is paler, isn't it?
- ❑ And the shape? Isn't it smaller?
- ❑ And the pain has actually decreased, hasn't it?

Yes, I think this is amazing. And I'd say, in about ninety-nine out of every one hundred tries, people notice a big difference. Did you?

The change in your back pain occurs for many reasons. One of them is that you are putting consciousness there, and that's the first step toward changing anything.

IT WORKS FOR ACTORS, IT CAN WORK FOR YOU

We're in the business of changing here—changing ourselves from a mass of tensions and insecurities into a body that feels good and free and relaxed so it will act how we want it to act. When you feel this way, that's when you'll give your best performance. That's when you really have a chance to be all you can be.

If you're having trouble visualizing a shape for your pain, or imagining yourself breathing white light into it, try this:

- ❑ Visualize a screen in front of your closed eyes.
- ❑ Imagine that the pain has a shape and voice of its own. On the screen. Maybe it looks like a bull, or a frog, or a tree. Or a little red Pac-Man who's furious.
- ❑ Get the image to speak to you, to tell you what the pain is about.

ALISSA MAKES THE BEST OF HER ANGER

ALISSA, A THIRTY-TWO-YEAR-OLD accountant who took one of my workshops, saw a little red Pac-Man on the screen in front of her closed eyes. He finally started screaming at her, "LEAVE YOUR JOB! LEAVE YOUR JOB!"

Alissa hated her job, and she'd been walking around with untold back pain for months—ever since she'd started the job, in fact.

Alissa started feeling better after she, herself, started screaming, "I HATE MY JOB! I HATE MY JOB!" And she felt even better when she left her job. She's now the book editor she always wanted to be. Bless her heart, she was just not cut out for accounting. And thank goodness she let herself hear the voice that was stuck, unheard in her, urging her to move on.

FEELING YOUR FEELINGS

THE SECOND PART of the Emotional Preparation, after you've presumably gotten yourself to where you're not conscious of your body feeling any tension or pain, is to ask yourself, very simply, "How am I feeling?"

- ❑ How *do* you feel right now?
- ❑ Try to speak your feelings out loud. I find that saying them aloud, and with my eyes closed, helps to intensify my experience of the feelings, whatever they are. Keeping your eyes closed somehow allows you to look more deeply inside to find out precisely what it is that you're feeling.
- ❑ If you're outside and there is a breeze, does it make you feel good?
- ❑ Or are you in a room that's too cold, and so you're a little angry?

- ❑ How do you feel about the chair you're sitting in? Does it need a more comfortable cushion? Or are you purring with joy to be in it?
- ❑ Has someone recently let you down, so you are sad?
- ❑ How do you feel about what you're going to be doing after you finish this exercise?
- ❑ How do you feel about whatever happened to you earlier today? Happy? Sad? Anxious? Afraid? Really explore how you feel.

If I had done that before I went into that audition so many years ago, I would have known how angry and hurt I was, and I could at least have done something with that pain and anger. At least I wouldn't have used up all my energy trying *not* to feel how I was feeling.

- ❑ If you don't know how you feel, it's okay. But now how does *that* make you feel, the fact that you don't know how you feel?
- ❑ Keep searching for the truth about how you feel.
- ❑ How do you feel about reading this book? The trick here is to know how you feel in the present moment. Now. In this moment that has never been before and will never be again. This moment where you're alive. So that you are as alive in this moment as you can be.
- ❑ If you think you might learn something from this book, does that excite you? Scare you?

HOW ACTORS FEEL THEIR FEELINGS

PROFESSIONAL ACTORS LEARN different ways to access and process their feelings. There are, of course, many ways to do this. Emotional workouts and catharses were a large and dramatic part of my early training.

At least six of my teachers had me lying on a classroom floor with other actors, all of us flailing our limbs at unseen enemies, crying in pain, or screaming out in anger. Lee Strasberg was the first teacher with whom I did a relaxation exercise where I got to cry and scream. Lee's students included James Dean, Marlon Brando, Paul Newman, Joanne Woodward, and Al Pacino. I alos did my fair share of crying and punching in a class with Larry Moss, whose students include Hilary Swank and Helen Hunt.

All of us, actors and non-actors, have to get those feelings out or we're blocked. We could even get sick. And we want to shine.

4

· Your Mental · Preparation

BEFORE I NEED to perform, after I've done my physical, vocal, and emotional warm-ups, I like to do the Mental Preparation.

Mental preparation will help you become more conscious of how your brain works, making you the sharp, intuitive thinker you want to be in every situation.

No one really knows precisely how to warm up the whole brain. Science is only just beginning to understand which part of the brain does what. But we can do something. So let's stir up that gray matter, access the parts of the brain that do some of the thinking. Give that brain a jolt; make sure it's as alive and functioning as it can be.

The following exercises are simple, but they work.

DOING SUMS

I DO SUMS. Seven plus fourteen. Fourteen plus twenty-eight. Just to wake up my brain. To make sure it's alive and awake. Twenty-eight plus seventy-two. If you're a whiz at math, pick harder numbers. Two thousand, four hundred and twenty-eight plus three thousand, four hundred and forty-nine.

It doesn't matter whether or not you come up with the right answers. The goal is to feel when and how and even where the brain is exercising in order for you to come up with what you hope are the right answers.

Can you feel your brain working?

Where exactly in the brain do you feel activity? Can you feel that computer in your head?

The first teacher I met who suggested a Mental Preparation like this was Paul Curtis, who taught "American Mime" in New York City. And I, along with Anita Morris and other actors you may or may not know, would walk around a room adding up my figures.

You don't have to walk and add up your figures. You can sit, or stand, or lie down. You can add and subtract and multiply and divide while driving in your car, if you want. Just as long as you don't get so carried away with the numbers that you forget you're in a car.

Patricia, a costume designer for television, finds that before production meetings, adding up figures makes her more focused and mentally alert than she would be if she didn't. Maybe because addition turns her on. Who cares why, just so long as she's awake when she walks into that meeting.

You can invent your own mental preparation, of course. Maybe algebra is your thing. Or deciphering Paleolithic petroglyphs. Maybe you can wake up that gray matter simply by reviewing the notes you made the night before for your presentation. Whatever works for you.

LETTERS OF THE ALPHABET

HERE'S ANOTHER MENTAL warm-up I like. It's simple, even silly, but you know how I feel about silly.

IT WORKS FOR ACTORS, IT CAN WORK FOR YOU

Silliness loosens you up, and even creates spaces inside of you where you didn't think you had any, so you have room to invent, and for things to move around and reinvent themselves. Silliness makes parts of you come alive that you didn't know existed, so that you can be all that you can be when you walk into a room.

So here's the exercise. It works for me. Think of all the words that begin with a certain letter of the alphabet. Say the letter "p."

Patina. Pulchritude. Palatial. Princely. Peculiar. Plump. Puppy. Pervasive.

Try the letter "v." Can you feel your brain, in a sense, searching for the words?

Feel it.

That's also what these exercises are for. Not only to get your brain working, but also to have you conscious of your brain working. So feel it, talk to it, get it to perform. Own it.

These exercises may be simple, but they do wake up your brain. And let's face it, when you have a presentation to give at eight o'clock in the morning, you want your brain to be awake.

Do whatever you have to do to get that computer humming. Maybe it's doing a crossword puzzle or remembering phone numbers from your childhood. Find out what works best for *you*. Again, the Mental Preparation is meant simply to get you conscious of your brain. So you walk into that meeting with your brain.

You don't want to show up unconsciously having left parts of you at home. If you bring only part of yourself into that meeting, people will sense that something is missing, if only unconsciously. Worse, so will you.

IT WORKS FOR ACTORS, IT CAN WORK FOR YOU

You want to walk into that meeting functioning on all cylinders, so don't leave your brain behind. Use some or all of these Mental Preparations to show up for that interview or that date as all you can be.

5

• Your Spiritual • Preparation

WHY IS IT that when some people walk into a room, everyone turns around to look at them? Why do some people shine? Why do some people seem to have a special light emanating from them? It's a special light. The stars in the sky have it. Movie stars have it. Marilyn Monroe. Robert Redford. Meryl Streep.

Eleonora Duse, considered by many to have been the greatest actress of the twentieth century, greater even than Sarah Bernhardt, was consistently described as "luminous." What is this light and where does it come from?

Duse, we know, worked at developing her spiritual life. In fact, she even stopped acting for several years and did nothing but pray and meditate. So it is not surprising that when she returned to the stage, she almost seemed to channel the light of the heavens through her body into her work.

We're talking about a measurable light here. Some people would say Duse had an exceptionally bright aura around her body. Sometimes it's called charisma. Saints are portrayed with halos. Those saints in those paintings have that light around them for a reason.

How can *you* add that extra dimension to how you look and feel? How can *you* get in touch with this abstract energy, an energy that is to some barely visible, to others, seemingly miraculous, mysterious, sublime, and divine?

One way is what I call the Spiritual Preparation. You say a prayer or do a meditation. Many actors do this before they go on stage. I am always impressed, watching the Broadway Tony Awards, by how many of the evening's winners thank God in their acceptance speeches.

SAY A LITTLE PRAYER

YOU DON'T HAVE to believe in God to be able to do this exercise. But if you do, just close your eyes and talk to whoever or whatever you think of as "God." Or leave your eyes open and talk to "God." Maybe thank him for whatever you are grateful for in your life, or tell him how you feel. Or ask for something you want. It's *your* relationship, you know what you can and cannot say.

When I talk to God before a performance, or anytime at all for that matter, I feel I come into a new, more profound place inside myself. I suddenly feel calm and centered in ways I didn't before. I feel newly at peace, even safe and loved.

IT WORKS FOR ACTORS, IT CAN WORK FOR YOU

Learning how to feel safe and loved at will is the perfect antidote to stage fright, both on stage and in everyday life.

After I pray, my work as an actress or teacher, my work, which is an extension of myself, tends to be richer, deeper, and more genuine.

For some people who work with me, this talking to God is all they need, before they go into a room, to feel centered and strong. Much as it did for the champion runner in the movie *Chariots of Fire*.

If your life does not include a relationship with God, there are many other options. You might try to find a miracle of Nature, anything that makes you feel the presence of a power greater than yourself. Maybe it's the ocean. Or a beautiful sunrise on a perfect summer day.

For one of my students, an agnostic pediatrician, a baby being born epitomized the miracle of life, of creation. The birth of a child was something the doctor couldn't logically comprehend, and of which he was in awe. For his prayer, he meditated on a baby's being born, felt himself there, saw, heard, and felt what he felt when he helped a child come into the world.

Let's say it's a waterfall that makes *you* feel that special sense of the splendor in the world:

- ❑ Try really *being* with that waterfall.
- ❑ Try and feel its spray.
- ❑ Sense the negative ions in the air.
- ❑ Smell them.
- ❑ Try to hear the water crashing against the rocks.
- ❑ Try to see it sparkling in the sunlight.
- ❑ Take a really deep breath of that special air.

How do you feel? As if you were really at the foot of that waterfall? Do you feel expanded from the experience? Changed? And if you were to go up to someone now, do you think he or she would see you as more shining than you were before you spent that time with the waterfall? I think so.

Because, miraculously, you temporarily borrow its light, its energy, its creative miracle and essence. You beam just as you might beam after having spent time at the real waterfall, or after having been inspired by some great painting, lecture, book, or movie, because your body has essentially been at that waterfall. By recreating its sensory aspects, the sight of it, its smell, and sound, your body is actually fooled into thinking it is there. (For a more detailed description of this phenomenon see chapter 7 on Sense Memory.)

In my workshops, after we all do this exercise, I have people go around the room and say their name. Usually when they do, their voices tend to be deeper, the timbre richer, and they seem not only to feel, but also to convey, a new sense of peace and centeredness that makes them feel safe and good. It's a wonderful place from which to enter a room and speak to anyone.

How does a prayer make *you* feel?

CONCHITA'S PRAYER

CONCHITA, A NURSE who took one of my workshops, was amazed that I included a spiritual preparation in my list of acting techniques. She was clearly moved, as well as thrilled, by how good she felt after her talk with God, because she had never thought of prayer as a tool to help her make her daily life richer. Somehow, she had thought of prayer as something she did only when she was in a church.

She had never thought of it as a practical tool to make her feel more alive. She had divorced God from her "ordinary" life, thinking God had no place in mundane matters. Her eyes were shining with relief when she thanked me for suggesting she use prayer in order to perform better, to give her the charge she needed at work for going from one hospital room to another.

It's a tool I actually do sometimes forget to use. And when I forget, I feel I cheat myself of riches that are my birthright. I always feel a hundred percent richer and more alive when I do put a prayer into my life, when I remember that I can experience the sacred in the ordinary.

Prayer centers many people, like me, and makes them calm and peaceful. Not unlike the way holy men are calm, peaceful, and centered. And holy men emanate light. Holy men have halos. Because they *do* shine. They pray and meditate, and whether they see the light, or feel it inside of them, it emanates from them and from the force of their prayer.

PRAYER REALLY DOES WORK

DR. STEPHEN STITELER monitors the effect of prayer and meditation on his patients with a process initially researched at Harvard University. He takes a drop of his patients' blood and lets them look at it under a microscope. Then he has them pray or meditate for five minutes. I did this, and the results were striking and impressive. Before prayer, my blood cells looked extremely coagulated bunched together as if in a traffic jam. Stiteler told me this state reduces oxygen distribution throughout the system.

The absence of oxygen can lead to cell fermentation, which as we also know, can lead to cancer. After my five minutes of prayer, however, my blood cells had spread out, as if they could breathe. No chance of cell fermentation there.

IT WORKS FOR ACTORS, IT CAN WORK FOR YOU

Prayer can help you feel calm, peaceful, and centered, which allows you to shine in any situation and light up any room you enter.

6

• Relaxation •

KONSTANTIN STANISLAVSKY, CONSIDERED by many to be the father of modern acting, spent many years studying the great actors of his time to discover the secret of their performances. This Russian genius and theater director attempted, like a scientist, to analyze what these great actors had in common, what it was that made them great, and what principles were at work in their performances. He wanted to teach what he discovered to the actors in his company, so they could be as strong, realistic, and brilliant as possible. And the actors of the Moscow Art Theater were.

Stanislavsky studied all the geniuses of his time, from Bernhardt to Salvini, and realized that what they all had in common was great relaxation. And for a long time, he believed that relaxation alone was the key to great acting. Even though, in later years, he realized that other elements were at least as important for a brilliant performance, neither he nor anyone I know disputes the absolute necessity of working from a state of relaxation.

For the first ten years of my acting career, when I was in New York, although I could play characters well and move audiences,

I was always upset by the fact that I could never cry on stage. Then I moved to California and started to study acting with Walter Lott, who had studied with Lee Strasberg, considered the father of Method acting, and who had himself studied Stanislavsky. Walter took one look at me, and said, "You need to learn how to relax." I did learn, and since then, I have to tell you, I've had no problem crying on stage. When I'm relaxed.

You are probably not interested in crying at will. But the lesson here is that if you're tense, then you're emotionally blocked.

IT WORKS FOR ACTORS, IT CAN WORK FOR YOU

Perhaps you've noticed that when you're tense, it's harder to perform. Your body doesn't move as easily, words don't come as quickly, and whatever you might want to express will be blocked in some way too, like your laughter, your spontaneity, and your creativity. One of the keys to putting your best self out there is learning to relax.

So, if there's anything you can do to relax, I say, "Do it."

Are your shoulders tense? Are they up around your ears? This is easy to achieve simply from driving a car. Or driving a cab. Or driving *in* a cab. Not to mention from hearing your job may be over. Those shoulders can literally start to strangle your neck. And then there's not a lot of blood and oxygen going up to your brain to help it to do all those things you want it to—like think and talk and be in control of your body.

Is your stomach in knots? Are your arms tight, so that they are even slightly pressing against your rib cage? This will not only limit the amount of oxygen that can get to your lungs, but also succeed in constricting all the organs behind your ribs, like your heart or your adrenals, both of which are probably shot anyway if you get easily scared.

So what do you do about it?

Every person's body is different. Everybody's synapses are connected to their own thoughts and history, so that everybody's wiring system is different. So that everybody needs to find their own special way to unknot the knots and relax the nerves, muscles, tendons, organs, and arteries.

Some people get terrible tension around their eyes, so that's where they have to concentrate in their relaxation. The trick is to find out what *your* body needs.

There are many ways to get your body to become as relaxed as it can be. Actually, every technique in this book is ideally a tool to bring you to greater relaxation. Not "fall-asleep relaxation," but that state of being where you have no unnecessary tension. The suggestions in this chapter may or may not work better for you than some other relaxation techniques that you already know—such as tensing your muscles very tight and then releasing them, which is often extremely effective. Every body is different.

I suggest you try all the relaxation ideas in this chapter. See which work best for you. One day one technique may work better than another, depending on what you've had for dinner or how angry you may be. It's just a matter of getting to know your "instrument," how it works and what makes it tick.

At the very least, if you try them all, your body and mind will get a freeing workout. You're training it, after all, to be as relaxed as possible. Many roads lead to Rome, and by doing all the exercises, you're showing your body not only how relaxed it can be, but also, hopefully, how good it can feel. And how else would you want to feel when you walk into that boardroom or singles mixer?

There are many ways to relax. A simple verbal command to your feet "to relax" or "let go" might do the trick. I use images because, in my experience, and for many people, they tend to allow the body to relax more deeply than if it were given a left brain verbal command. An image or visualization, entered into your brain, often has more impact on your body than words because it enters a more primal area of the psyche. Try some of the images below. If they don't work for you, you can always go back to words.

The trick here, of course, is that you are becoming conscious of an area of your body, and when it is given attention and focus, it will automatically relax. It's the same consciousness that performed healing miracles in the Emotional Preparation, when you imaged your pain having a color and a shape, and then breathed a different-colored light into the shape, and not only watched the shape and color change, but also felt the pain dissipate. Remember, tension is only a more subtle form of pain.

IMAGING FOR YOUR FEET

I ALWAYS START with the feet.

- ❑ Try moving your toes around. Or just be conscious of them.
- ❑ I personally like to imagine that the balls of my feet are like the soft pads on the paws of a big cat: kind of relaxed and a little mushy. For me, using an image like this is even more powerful for relaxing my feet than moving them around.
- ❑ Sometimes, I'll thank the bottoms of my feet for carrying me around all day. I'll acknowledge how much work they do and how important they are to me, helping me to "stand on my own two feet." Ideas move me. Gratitude moves me. When I'm "moved," I can feel another movement occur, a change as I relax a little more into my body and somehow let go of some of the tension I've been holding.
- ❑ Now, focus on the bones of the foot, your toes, and five metatarsals. Imagine the spaces in the joints to be expanding as you focus on them, so there will be extra space between all the different bones. So there is more room in those feet when you walk around on them.

IT WORKS FOR ACTORS, IT CAN WORK FOR YOU

Do you feel you're not taking up as much space on this planet as you were meant to take up? Then start with your feet: how wonderful to have a support system with more breadth, height, and width than before you relaxed!

- ❑ Now focus on the arch of your left foot. Imagine it's the arc of a rainbow. Can you see the red, orange, yellow, green, blue, indigo, and violet? Now expand that rainbow's arc with your breath. Can you see it expanding? Can you feel it?
- ❑ Now do your right foot.

ANKLES, CALVES, KNEES, AND THIGHS

- ❑ Now focus on your ankles. Pretty important, those ankles. They move us forward. If we're not moving forward, we could stagnate and die.
- ❑ Try and move into the spaces between those bones and fill them with light, until the whole ankle area expands with breath, so you and it become more flexible. Try white light. Try green light. Experiment with other colors. One day, red may work better for you, another day, blue. All colors have healing properties. Trust your intuition to know what color you may need on any given day.
- ❑ Now focus on the calf. It almost doesn't matter what images you use, once you know which images work. For the calf, you might imagine its two bones are white, shining arrows, and see yourself aiming them at whatever you want in your life, whether it's relaxation, a job, or a dream of yourself being brilliant in some presently difficult social situation.
- ❑ You might try thinking of the fleshy part of the calf as

molasses melting into the waffle of the rug. Yes, that's when you're relaxing on the floor. For me, relaxation exercises are easiest if I'm lying down. I relax better lying down than sitting or standing up. I figure that's why it's easier for me to fall asleep lying down than standing or sitting. Of course, you can always do the relaxation in a chair.

- ❑ So, your calves are melting into the floor—like molasses, or melted butter, or syrup or anything that lets you feel those calf muscles relax.
- ❑ Move up to the knee. Try to imagine that your knee is a flower in a time-lapse photograph. Your favorite flower. And watch the petals unfold. So there's extra light between all the spaces in the knee. The more light you imagine shining inside of you, the more you will shine. Charisma 101.

Don't cheat yourself on that knee joint, that delicate, complicated combination of bones and tendons and ligaments and a ball and a socket. Your knee is the part of you that moves forward first, whenever you walk, so you want it always to be flexible, so you can move forward as easily and effortlessly as you may ever need or want to.

Some theories state that our knees vibrate with our needs, so just in case that's true, I sure as hell want *mine* to be healthy and fulfilled. So go for it, really light up that flower. Move as much light, oxygen, and consciousness into its spaces as you can.

- ❑ Your thighbones are the biggest, heaviest bones in your body. Feel their weight, their power. This exercise is really about truly owning your body, experiencing it from the inside as well from the outside. Try thinking of your thighbone as some gargantuan Neanderthal club that you can use to get you what you want. I say use any exercise you can to get in touch with your power.
- ❑ As for the flesh of your thighs, have them melt into the floor with whatever image works best for you. Melted butter into

the toast of the rug? Hot fudge or raspberry syrup onto the pound cake of the floor?

YOUR ANUS AND GENITALS

- ❑ Focus on your anus. Yes, your anus.
- ❑ Is it tight, holding? Amazing isn't it. A lot of people hold tension there, and that holding simply blocks so much creative energy from flowing up and down the spine.
- ❑ Relax your anus. You might try tightening it, so you can relax it even more.

IT WORKS FOR ACTORS, IT CAN WORK FOR YOU

These relaxation exercises are as much about awareness as anything else. Only after awareness (or consciousness) is change possible. And that's the gift, challenge, and triumph of the actor, this ability to change and even totally transform himself. You can use these exercises to do the same for yourself.

- ❑ Focus on your genitals.
- ❑ Send some light in there. Try red. Feel the strength of your reproductive organs.
- ❑ If you're a man, feel the force of your sperm, their ability to create. To make things grow. You are creating a new you, here, at the very least, in certain situations. When you give your sperm a hit of red light, do you feel extra power? Do you think you could become more potent by sending red light to your sperm? Why not? Be born again here.
- ❑ And if you're a woman, go ahead and send some light to those ovaries. And if your eggs have dwindled, to where they

were. Your body remembers what that space is for. Light up those eggs. What self do *you* want to give birth to?

WHY SHOULD YOU WORK WITH LIGHT?

LIGHT IS A healing energy. If you lock someone in a dark room for a week without it, you can monitor and even measure their depression.

We all know what happens to a plant without light.

And there are healers out there who consciously use light to make sick people well—Reiki practitioners, among others. There are even special machines that beam colors onto the sick parts of peoples' bodies, or full spectrum light to help turn around the depression caused by seasonal affective disorder (SAD).

If you want to shine, you have to get in touch with light, and become aware of its power and grace.

On a stage or on a movie set, good actors always know, almost instinctively, how to find their light. And it's not only the light overhead.

YOUR TORSO

- ❑ Focus your attention on your intestinal tract. Image it as a clean, shining hose.
- ❑ Send even more light to it, to all those yards and yards of intestines, to help your digestion, not only of the food you ate today, but also of any thoughts and ideas you may need to digest: from something you read today, or from something in this book.
- ❑ Now, visualize your spine. See and feel each vertebra as a fancy-cut diamond, sparkling in a necklace down the center of your body. Breathe white shining light, also, into the spaces between the vertebrae.

- ❏ Now, breathe into your lungs. Fill the diaphanous sacks with cool air. They are wet all the time, did you know that? Feel them. Acknowledge the miracle of how they work, and how you couldn't live without them, as they allow you to take in the breath of life, so that you feel alive. Because it's your alive and shining self that you want to bring out onto that stage, wherever it is.
- ❏ Try giving a hit of light to your liver, sitting under the bottom of your right rib cage. The liver, it is said, holds our anger. Feel it. Breathe in white light. Let out the angry, noxious fumes. Energize it so you can use your anger to get what you want. To change.
- ❏ Improvise. Maybe do your spleen, or your gallbladder. Be inventive. Focus on an artery, a vein, a muscle, a tendon. Cells. Mitochondria. Whatever turns you on.

FROM YOUR HEART TO YOUR HEAD

- ❏ Now concentrate on your heart. Feel it beating. It's your heartbeat. A sign you're alive. Your heart keeps you alive. Feel it beat, follow its rhythms.
- ❏ Image a warm red light around your heart, cushioning it.
- ❏ Feel your heart area expand inside you. We love from our hearts. Can you feel your love for others? Your love for yourself? Your loving all the veins and arteries where your blood is flowing? Your loving yourself for wanting and daring to be more alive and perform better in your life?
- ❏ Let the warm red light in your heart cavity, pulsing with blood and energy, flow through your arms, and out through your hands and fingertips, till the joints are alive and expanding with ruby red energy.
- ❏ Feel your arms, your hands, and your fingers come alive, ready to embrace what you want, hug whom you want. Feel

your hands ready to shake someone else's hand, or feed you, or give gifts, or receive money.

- ❏ Test how much harder it is to feel anything if your fingers and hands are clenched. Tighten them and then feel some piece of clothing. Now relax them and feel the same clothing, and feel how much more you feel.

Do anything that relaxes you. If it's feeling your fingernails growing, feel them growing. If it's feeling the blood coursing through your veins, do that.

- ❏ Now focus on your neck, the creative center of the body, which you've presumably already woken up in the physical warm-up. Feel your neck muscles to be as relaxed as lasagna noodles, if that image gets your muscles to relax. The lasagna noodles usually work for me. Of course they sometimes make me hungry, and I'll want to go out for Italian food. But I love it, and I feel great eating it, and alive and full afterward—so the relaxation's working.
- ❏ Now for your head: Try to imagine an explosion of fireworks in your mandibular joint, so your mouth can open more fully.
- ❏ Maybe it will help you if you stretch your mouth open wide. Or if you make sounds, any sounds you might feel like making. Laugh, cry, scream, whimper like a baby. Or just enjoy your mouth relaxing.
- ❏ Focus next on the muscles around your eyes. Feel them relax. Imagine gentle fingers tapping all around them, and at the temples, where the blue nerves are, the nerves that give us headaches when they're tense.
- ❏ Focus on your eyes. Imagine that they're oysters, limp in their shells (your sockets). Hate oysters? Try raw eggs. Sick of food? Try mercury. Or a pebble in a pond. Find an image that works for you. Or just hear yourself saying, "I'm relaxing my eyes. My eyes are warm and heavy now. I'm relaxing my eyes."

- ❑ Feel your forehead. Try to imagine a cool hand soothing the wrinkles on your brow, ironing out the space between your eyebrows and your hairline. When you get up from the relaxation, look at your face in a mirror and notice that some of the worry lines are gone. (This relaxation is cheaper than a face-lift, and unquestionably more fun.)
- ❑ Now relax your brain. Breathe new light and spaces between the cerebellum, the thalamus, the brain stem, and the medulla—wherever you imagine them to be, between anything you can imagine in there.
- ❑ Focus on the muscles around the scull. Relax them.
- ❑ Finally, focus on your hair. Yes, your hair. Which according to ancient mystical traditions, is made up of filaments growing to God. So, feel them growing.

We often take our hair for granted, but those hairs keep growing even after we're dead! Even after our hearts have stopped, and our brains have stopped working. Those hairs know something we don't know. So feel their special aliveness. Relax the places where they attach to your skull.

A SHIELD TO PROTECT YOURSELF

Can you visualize your hair as filaments of light extending from your head like a halo? We're back to your charisma, your ability to let the light inside of you shine out of you. Let your hairs be part of that letting out of light.

Now let the light from your hair fall down your face, neck, shoulders, back, and legs, until it encases your whole body, as if it were a cocoon. Let this cocoon of white light protect your relaxed and open body, keeping in your relaxation, keeping out anything negative, anything that might upset you. Anyone can build this invisible shield. Can you feel yours?

Slowly, at your own pace, come back to the room. Wiggle your fingers and toes. Move your hands and feet. Slowly open your eyes.

Notice, as you begin to focus, that after relaxing, you actually see colors more vividly, the outlines of objects more clearly. You actually *see* more clearly! This amazing perception is all I need to realize how important relaxation is. How can we be at our best in *any* situation, if we can't see what's going on around us?

PERFORMING AND RELAXING AT THE SAME TIME

TWO OF MY teachers, John Lehne and Sandra Seacat, who both studied with Lee Strasberg, emphasized a wonderful relaxation technique in their classes. While we were doing a scene, they had us consciously think, "Are my shoulders up?" or "Is my anus tight?" or "Am I holding tension in my hip?" Just the question would allow my shoulders to go down, my arms to relax, or my hip to release.

John was Jill Clayburgh's teacher, and Sandra taught Jessica Lange, Mickey Rourke, and Treat Williams. Watch these actors' movies and see how relaxed they are.

So if you're at a difficult business meeting, tune into your body for a minute. Try and sense where you may be tense. Tell yourself to relax that tension. At the very least, you will look as if you were thinking. If you achieve that state of relaxation that these exercises can create for you, you will be able to perform without physical tension, have access to a voice and emotions that you can control, and be fully present, both mentally and spiritually. This is of course the state in which every actor longs to find himself for every performance. See if it doesn't also work for you.

· Nuts-and-Bolts · Techniques

PART TWO

This section *includes some of the most basic and well-known acting techniques used today, including Sense Memory, Substitution, Playing a Character, and the Psycho-Physical Action.*

They can all be exciting to use and fun to try. Some of their results may surprise and even shock you, because you may find that they push your imagination to the limits, allowing you to behave in ways you never thought you could and think and say things you never dared to before.

7

• Sense Memory •

SENSE MEMORY IS one of the most basic and most effective acting techniques for improving real-life situations. Not only is it used in one form or another by most actors, but it is also the basis for a great number of other acting techniques.

Sense Memory is one of the techniques that allows an actor to laugh or cry on a dime—sometimes simply by remembering the smell of someone's perfume, or the taste of a special dessert.

What you do is remember something with your senses. The smell of a rose. The touch of someone's hand on your cheek. Your whole body will react as if the rose or hand were really there because our bodies have stored every sensory experience we have ever had.

DISCOVER SENSE MEMORY WITH A LEMON WEDGE

- ❑ With your eyes open or closed, imagine you are holding a lemon wedge and *see* its bright yellow color.
- ❑ *Feel* its thick nubby skin.

- ❑ Bring your hand with the imaginary lemon in it toward your face, and with a deep breath *smell* the lemon.
- ❑ Now bring the lemon wedge toward your teeth and *feel* your teeth against the translucent membrane.
- ❑ Bite into the lemon and *feel* your teeth as they move through the membrane and the pulp.
- ❑ *Feel* the juice as it begins to run into your mouth. Feel it on your tongue, and on your teeth and gums. What temperature is it? Is it cold? Warm?
- ❑ How does it *taste*? Is it sweet? Is it sour? Bitter?

Are you salivating now? You probably are. Roughly ninety-nine out of every one hundred people who work with me do. Why? Because our unconscious body memories do not know the difference between what is real and what is imaginary. Everything we have ever sensed with our bodies is stored in the amazing computer that is our brain, and simply by ordering one of your senses to remember some sensory reality, your body will react as if the sensory stimulus were really there.

The ramifications of this physical phenomenon are far-reaching and really thrilling. Let's face it: there was no real lemon, and you were salivating, which is an unconscious physical response, like stage fright with its sweaty palms, dry mouth, and hyperventilation. People can scream "SALIVATE!" to you until the cows come home, but if you don't actually imagine a taste, a feel, or a smell, you won't.

IT WORKS FOR ACTORS, IT CAN WORK FOR YOU

If you want your body to be relaxed, playful, or powerful, the trick is to know what sensory reality actually makes your body *feel* relaxed, playful, powerful, or anything else you might want it to feel. You can use Sense Memory to get there.

Sensory stimuli affect us all the time. If you suddenly remember someone who has died, whom you loved, you will unconsciously remember some sensory detail about that person—his smell, the sound of his laugh, the light in his eye, and your whole body and mood will change. Your whole body and mood change with even the subtlest change in either your physical reality or your memory of a physical reality.

If it is raining, if you have a stomachache, if you go to the circus, or if you can remember a particular rain, stomachache, or circus, your whole body will change. Suddenly you are happy or sad or silly or thoughtful. Actors consciously create, or rather recreate, these remembered states and transform themselves into characters who are happy, sad, silly, thoughtful, or anything else.

HOW SENSE MEMORY WORKS FOR ME

THE CRASHING OF ocean waves on rocks makes my body feel alive and powerful and safe. Real ocean waves, or the same waves recreated sensorily. In other words, *hearing* the crashing of the waves, *smelling* the salty sea air, *seeing* the foam, all these sensory realities make my body act as if it were really at the ocean, whether I'm there or not. And I just feel wonderful.

You could say it's a cheap high. It's certainly a way for me to control my body, instead of having my body make me feel something else—tense, unhappy, or scared. I like feeling relaxed, powerful, and excited. So, in a situation where I might otherwise be feeling tense, pathetic, or slightly dead, recreating the crashing ocean waves on the wall opposite me is just what I need to have a good time.

MARILYN MONROE USED SENSE MEMORY

SIR LAWRENCE OLIVIER directed Marilyn Monroe in the movie *The Prince and The Showgirl*. He wanted her to enter her first scene sparkling and full of spunk and wit. To his great frustration, none of his directions, ideas, explanations, or demonstrations seemed to help at all.

Then Marilyn's acting coach, Paula Strasberg, told her to use "Coca-Cola and Frankie Sinatra."

That was all she needed. She tasted the Coca-Cola, felt the bubbles, heard the fizz. She heard Sinatra's voice, saw his face, felt his hand, his arm, whatever. And she is scintillating in that scene. Simply by using Sense Memory.

HOW *YOU* CAN USE SENSE MEMORY

LET'S SAY YOU have a job interview, and you're nervous. If you feel great about that interview, just walk in there, have a good time, and get that job.

But let's say you're nervous. The trick here is to find those Sense Memories that will make you feel however you want to feel when you walk into that room.

What makes *you* feel confident, loved, and alive? If it's your lover, use your lover. If it's your dog, use your dog. And use all five senses to recreate every detail that you can: skin color; the look in the eye; the colors of the eye; the tone of the voice; the smell.

Be as specific as possible. That's your preparation before you go into that interview. Eventually, you may find that just one sensory detail will trigger your body's total transformation.

If there's some one-ring circus that makes you feel wonderful and secure, then smell the popcorn and the elephants. Feel the cotton candy, sticky around your mouth. Taste how sweet it is on your tongue. Feel the hardness of the circus bench underneath you. And when you go into that interview, bring your circus with you:

- ❑ When you look up at the ceiling, see the red and blue stripes of the circus tent over your head, if that's what convinces your body that you're actually there.

- ❑ Or see your favorite ballerina on the flying trapeze.
- ❑ Can you imagine your favorite bareback rider rearing her horse right behind whoever is interviewing you?
- ❑ What about the largest bag of popcorn possible, sitting on your lap?

IT WORKS FOR ACTORS, IT CAN WORK FOR YOU

Dustin Hoffman says he'll use absolutely anything on a set to get him to be however he needs to be. It should be no different for us in real life. Use Sense Memory to make you feel how *you* want to feel, and no one will even know what you're doing.

Someone I know can go into a meeting and only has to think when he sits down that he is sitting on that circus bench, and he's relaxed and happy. And he can sustain those feelings all the way through the meeting, no matter what surprise questions he may have to field.

What if you feel your circus excitement at the beginning of the interview, but you lose it later on, and suddenly notice yourself getting dry-mouthed and tense?

Just send in the clowns. Hear the outrageous honk of a rubber horn, if that brings back your circus high. Hear it just for a minute, to relax you, center you, make you come alive. Or, with a deep breath, breathe in the smell of the sawdust. Then go back to being interviewed.

Don't be afraid of taking that moment. What's the worst thing your interviewer could be thinking? Could he be thinking that you're thinking? You are! And he probably wants to hire somebody who thinks. Smelling the sawdust will only take a second; and probably no one but you will even notice that you are doing anything out of the ordinary.

What you are doing is waking up and bringing yourself into your secure, happy body, instead of drowning in some unconscious scenario of when you were scared as a kid. Your interviewer is going to want to hire someone who is secure and happy. Go for it.

SENSE MEMORY EXERCISES

HOW DO YOU want to feel and what makes you feel that way? Does the ocean make you feel excited and alive, or does it make you want to go to sleep? If it makes you want to go to sleep, this is not the Sense Memory you want to use before going into that high-powered business meeting.

For situations where you might feel uncomfortable, what would make you feel safe? A favorite tree? A certain running brook? The view outside your bedroom window? Whatever it is that makes you feel how you want to feel, the technique is the same: You create the situation sensorily and ask yourself specific questions:

- ❑ What are you *seeing*? Be as specific as possible. What is the exact color of what you are seeing? Can you be even more specific about the shade?
- ❑ What are you *hearing*? Is there a special piano piece that makes you smile? Who's playing it? How rich is the tone of the piano?
- ❑ What are you *feeling* against your body? Again make sure you force your body to feel it by asking specific questions: If it's fur, is it as soft as your dog's, or not as soft as your rabbit's?
- ❑ What are you *smelling*? Again, be specific. If you're recreating the smell of a rose, it might help you to ask what else the rose smells like to get you to focus. For example: Is it like vanilla, or cloves? Or pancake batter?
- ❑ What is your favorite food? Be specific and describe exactly what you are tasting. How sweet is that sundae? Describe the exact texture of the hot fudge; try and sense precisely how hot it is, how cold the ice cream.

- ❑ What is your favorite animal? Does your dog make you smile? Does she smell like popcorn? Can you see the dirt on her nose?

If you have a favorite beach or mountaintop that inspires you, *feel* the wind there, its temperature, its speed, its softness. Or does it almost burn your face? If it feels good, use it. If pain turns you on, use it.

If a certain garden makes you smile, really *smell* the air. Be specific. Does it smell like something else? Like peaches? Or talcum powder? Or your grandmother? If not, how is it different?

IT WORKS FOR ACTORS, IT CAN WORK FOR YOU

The more you are conscious of the sensory specifics, the less your attention will be on your nerves or on how badly you may be doing. Instead of focusing on the judges who aren't really there, you will be focused on a positive experience that will get you smiling.

So, if you're at the ocean:

- ❑ Can you really *hear* the waves? Do they sound like drums? Or cymbals?
- ❑ Can you hear birds? *Really* hear them? Breathe. Listen again.
- ❑ Can you *feel* your skin? Is someone touching it? With how soft a touch?
- ❑ Is someone sitting next to you? Is she wearing a bikini? What color is it?
- ❑ Is the man next to you wearing anything at all? What color is it?

Find what turns you on and bring it into those difficult situations. No one but you will know if you bring in an imaginary big hairy sheepdog to that high-powered lunch. But if that mutt makes you feel secure, you just put that doggy under the table. Let him do anything he wants. Anything. This will relax you, and give you a focus for your attention other than whether the man across the table likes you.

You don't need these techniques, remember, if the job interview is somehow automatically or magically easy. But sometimes, just a hint of something you love, the sound of your favorite song, the taste of your favorite food, will reprogram your unconscious from a state of fear into a state of joy, and then it's easy sailing.

IT WORKS FOR ACTORS, IT CAN WORK FOR YOU

If some unconscious tape is getting you scared, replace it with a Sense Memory. Remember, you're contacting your unconscious when you do. Replace the lousy tape with a good one, one that makes you feel great.

SENSE MEMORY REALLY DOES WORK

DR. CHERYL KLEEFELD, licensed psychologist and Fellow of the Biofeedback Certification Institute of America, tells me that she uses "sensory imagery" all the time to help people bring down levels of pain, blood pressure, and anxiety. "Sensory imagery" is one of the medical terms for Sense Memory.

"Sense Memory is actually an old concept in the field of psychotherapy," Dr. Kleefeld relates. "It dates back to Pavlovian conditioning, where neutral stimuli are paired with unconditioned stimuli to bring about a conditioned response. Sense Memory is a variation of this type of training, which brings involuntary, autonomic physiological processes under conscious control."

Belleruth Naparstek, an expert and best-selling author on the subject of "guided imagery" (another name for Sense Memory), cites a number of studies demonstrating the power of Sense Memory. Here are two.

In 2000, researchers at Beth Israel Deaconess Medical Center in Boston and Elvira Lang at Harvard Medical School studied 241 people having invasive, high-anxiety surgeries that did not require general anesthesia but only topical pain medication. Of the three groups studied, the first was given technical information from their doctor, before the operation, on what would happen; the second group was given a nurse coach who sat by the patients' heads giving both information and reassurance (in other words, "You're doing great").

The third group was given a nurse coach who led the patients in sensory, guided imagery. This group tested with lower pain levels, shorter hospital stays, and had significantly less anxiety than the other two groups.

Naparstek also participated in a study at the University of California, Davis, with Henry David, where patients heard audiotapes during their operations. Of the four groups studied, the first group was played tones that drive the brain into a state of relaxation; the second group was given cognitive information ("Here's what to expect"); the third group was played affirmations to music.

The fourth group was given Naparstek's *Guided Sensory Imagery* tape. This group reduced the length of its patients' hospital stays by twenty-eight hours, had significantly less blood loss (150cc less), had less reported anxiety, and less postoperative pain than the other three groups.

In other words, when people use the proper Sense Memory, their bodies can get stronger and their anxiety levels diminish.

A PRACTICAL QUESTION YOU MAY BE ASKING

My clients sometimes ask, "Won't I be distracted from my conversation—say, with the bank president, if I am feeling some dog pounding my leg with its head? Don't I need my total attention on that conversation?"

Yes, you do. What you don't need are all of your fears, all of your tensions, and all those mental knots and paranoid fantasies that can also show up at times like this. In many ways, the right Sense Memory can melt them away.

The truth is, if you are hearing some negative tape, based on something negative that was done to you in the past, you will not be fully with the man across the desk anyway. Better you should be with an imaginary dog that makes you feel good, than with some unconscious memory of your father yelling at you making you think you did something bad. And as you have seen, whether it's a real dog or an imaginary dog, your body will react in the same positive way. It's just sometimes not real convenient to bring a real, big, shaggy sheepdog with you to a formal business meeting.

Sense Memory doesn't have to distract you from the conversation at hand, any more than if your favorite dog were really lying across your feet or if your favorite flowers were really on that desk. And if you really love that dog, if he really makes you feel relaxed and happy, you might perform even better if he *were* there.

In my workshops I have people hold a stone in their hand and say, "I am Amanda Petunia"—or whatever their name is—"and I am feeling this stone in my hand and I can see you and hear you and talk to you at the same time." This allows people to realize that *feeling* the stone in their hands really doesn't diminish their ability to hear, talk, see, and do what they have to do.

Try it. You'll see.

A SCREENWRITER USES SENSE MEMORY

JACK, A THIRTY-FIVE-YEAR-OLD television writer, was an amusing man. I'd met him at one of his plays. He was warm, personable, and funny—like the protagonist of his comedy.

He came to me because he had trouble doing what is known in show business as "pitching stories," that is, selling ideas for shows and movies to rooms full of television executives. In the network building boardrooms, he would freeze. His mouth went dry; he couldn't think. Not only did his humor leave him, and his charm, but also his words.

I explained the premise of Sense Memory to him. We tried to find something he could use. The ocean didn't work. His favorite foods didn't work.

I knew that Jack was married, and he mentioned he had recently had a little girl. As soon as he told me her name, his face lit up. He came alive, was clearly relaxed, and felt good.

I asked him to imagine his little girl on his lap. He immediately started smiling, practically laughing. We know that when we smile, we actually emit a chemical that strengthens our immune systems, so that at the same time Jack was having a good time thinking about his daughter, his body was getting stronger—which is of course what he wanted to feel at those pitch meetings.

Without even trying, Jack could instantly *smell* his daughter's hair, *hear* her laugh, *feel* her skin, *see* her face. I suggested that he go into his pitch meetings doing a Sense Memory of his little girl on his lap.

Sometimes, I work with people for weeks or even months, until they learn to relax and can go into meetings or social situations being how they want to be.

With Jack, it took one session. As soon as we came up with the idea of his little girl, it was clear he wouldn't need anything else. Just the thought of her and he was smiling, his body felt safe, his humor had returned.

Jack's loving feelings were stronger than his fear, and the Sense Memory went right to his unconscious, and in a sense reprogrammed his brain to feel love and security instead of stage fright and angst.

Jack not only talks at those pitch meetings now, he actually enjoys them.

8

• Substitution •

SUBSTITUTION IS A specialized use of Sense Memory, and is, in fact, the act of substituting one sensory reality for another, in other words, of turning anything unpleasant into something wonderful. And your body will believe it's wonderful, since you've tricked it by using Sense Memory.

Here's an example of how Substitution saved my life.

Movie cameras used to terrify me. Not a good thing for an actress who wanted to be in movies. I used to fear the camera as if it were a machine gun out to get me. They are, after all, big, black, and metal. Movie cameras scared me until I figured out how to substitute other objects for the camera. Sensorily.

I started with black dogs. I love black dogs. Actually, I also love white dogs, brown dogs, and spotted dogs, but cameras are black, so I went for black. I pretended that the camera was some Lab or poodle or scruffy black mutt, and my fear of the camera would disappear.

I would imagine the dog's smell and bark. I would imagine the glint in his eye. I would hear him pant, even imagine him slobbering all over the cameraman, or me. So the camera became a friend, not some secret enemy out to get me. Dogs relax me, and make me feel comfortable and loved. Which is how I want to be feeling if I'm acting in front of a camera.

I'm not saying that I put myself into some hallucinogenic trance. I don't get kibble for the camera and start petting it—though one actress I know goes up to the camera before a shoot and hugs it. As if this ritual will neutralize it for her and turn her and the camera into friends. Which it seems to do.

Sometimes, if I get tired of dogs, I will substitute the eye of someone I love for the eye of the camera. I was dating a very loving man with black hair and dark eyes for a while, and substituting *him* really did the trick. (Until we broke up.)

One of my favorite substitutions is Talia Shire, the actress who played Stallone's girlfriend in the *Rocky* movies, not only because she has intense dark eyes, but also, and more importantly, because I feel she respects me, and I respect her. So I'm happy to imagine her eye in or behind the camera. When she directed her first film, *One Night Stand*, and cast me in it, her amazing eyes literally were behind the camera. And then I didn't need to use any Substitution at all.

A BLIND DATE

LINDA, A THIRTY-YEAR-OLD graphic designer, got so tense on blind dates that she could hardly speak. So we worked up an arsenal of substitutions that she could use for these potentially horrendous rituals. The sensory substitution would dispel whatever paranoid projections were at work on her blind dates. It wasn't as though she were going out with guys from the Mob, who might be hiding machine guns in their pockets.

If the blind date included a meal in a restaurant, she would substitute her favorite flowers, yellow freesias, for any flowers that might be on the table. She would smell the freesias, imagine seeing the specific shape of their delicate green stems, the exact yellow of the flowers themselves.

She understood she had to be as specific as possible to make her substitution as vivid as she could, so that she could get to her unconscious as immediately as possible, to change the tape that might ordinarily be running, scaring her frozen. So she could stop the tape that went something like: "Oh, my God, I'm scared! My whole life depends on this dinner! If he doesn't like me, I'll die. Because surely, this man will take care of me for the rest of my life. My very survival depends on him."

This is an old tape from Linda's childhood, one that she had had to create as a little girl in order to survive in a house where a dangerous, raging father had succeeded in scaring her into silence.

By giving herself those flowers, with her body reacting to those flowers, Linda was tricking her unconscious into playing a tape that went more like this: "Oh, look, look! Someone has just brought me the most beautiful flowers, my favorites! That someone is me. I do not depend on this man for survival. I can depend on *myself* for survival. Look how happy I am now, with my favorite flowers. I am happy now and feeling safe and loved, and therefore can be more myself."

IT WORKS FOR ACTORS, IT CAN WORK FOR YOU

You can change your mood and brain chemistry with a simple Substitution, which means you actually get to *choose* if you want to feel good or bad. Try to remember this whenever you're feeling bad.

In case Linda wanted to use another Substitution, I asked her what music she loved. She was particularly fond of a certain lullaby by Schumann. She said it always made her smile. She practiced hearing it in her head, played by her favorite pianist, and felt her whole body relax and smile as she did. She could substitute her Schumann melody for the noise in the restaurant.

Linda's arsenal also included her own kitchen door, which she could substitute for the kitchen door of whatever restaurant she might find herself with her date. Because her own kitchen door made her smile. She always felt safe in her kitchen. Because she was a wonderful cook, and always felt creative there and powerful there.

Chapter 7 on Sense Memory scientifically explains how effective Sense Memory can be. Even Marcel Proust in his masterpiece, *Remembrance of Things Past,* understood that the slightest sensory detail (in his case, a thin sugar cookie) could transform a body's entire sense of being.

I worked with Linda on how to recreate that kitchen door, with as many specific sensory details as possible. She saw the door's white, speckled paint, and the place where its wood was a little warped. She saw the metal of its hinges, their exact color and shine. Not that she would have to go through all these details once she got to the restaurant, but so that she would find which detail most quickly brought the door to life for her.

We talked about her substituting her favorite smell from her kitchen for whatever smells might be in the restaurant. Her fresh hot cross buns seemed to do it for her, right when they were ready to be taken out of the oven.

So on her date when the waiter brought the bread to the table, she could imagine her own famous hot cross buns in the basket. By substituting them for the bread on the table, Linda was, in effect, fooling her body into thinking she was in an entirely safe environment—in other words, home, and her body relaxed as if it were totally safe. She felt cared for and loved, which she was—by herself. And this way, she wasn't desperate for her blind date to satisfy all her needs for care, closeness, tenderness, safety, and loving—on the first date.

THE ACTRESS WAS A WAITRESS

ACTORS, TOO, HEIGHTEN their reality when they have to. Sometimes an actor has to get really excited about a situation in a play or a movie, and the situation in the play or the movie just isn't that exciting to the actor. That's when the actor will substitute another situation for the situation in the script.

Let's say an actress is given a part in a movie in which she has to run into a room totally thrilled, because she had just gotten a job as a waitress in a restaurant. Now let's say this actress has already been a waitress in a restaurant. For more years than she wants to remember. And the prospect of ever waitressing again is about as appealing to her as finding a frog in her soup.

But in the movie she has to burst into this room, and be excited as all get out that she's gotten this job as a waitress.

So maybe she won't use the circumstances of the script. Maybe she'll substitute the "good news" of the script for what would be good news for her. Like winning the lottery and buying all the things she can't actually afford to buy, like new clothes, a sailboat, and a financial independence that would mean she'd never have to waitress again.

Substituting that sailboat for that waitress job could very well do the trick for our actress. She could sensorily create new clothes or the sailboat of her dreams. Maybe just the words "winning the lottery," or the thought that she would have all that money in the bank would do it. For some people, words, thoughts, and ideas can be as stimulating as sensory stimuli. What about for you?

9

• Personalization •

PERSONALIZATION IS A variation of Sense Memory and Substitution, and is what you might guess it to be. In Personalization, you transform, sensorily, a person with whom you might be *un*comfortable, into a person with whom you know you *are* comfortable.

So, who's *your* best friend, and how can you hang out with her or him when you're with someone who makes you uncomfortable? Who is the person with whom you feel you're most relaxed and comfortable, the person with whom you feel you can most be your favorite, fullest self? Who's the person with whom you're relaxed enough to joke or be smart, with whom thinking and talking and sharing is easy, with whom your true best self comes shining through? That best friend is the person you want to substitute for the boss who makes you nervous, or the school principal who makes you uptight. And that's called Substitution.

MY BEST FRIEND

ANNA NORBERG IS *my* best friend, and has been since we went to college together. Maybe because we had more goofy, outrageous adventures there than a barrel of monkeys. We're still in touch with each other, even though we now live two thousand miles apart.

If I notice that someone is making me nervous—at a job interview, in a restaurant, on a bus—I'll turn that person into Anna Norberg. If I can remember to do that. I don't always remember. I get scared and I forget. Or I get cocky and forget. Or I just forget. (I hate when forgetting is just another word for self-sabotage.)

If I remember to use Personalization, my life can be so much easier. Because my body doesn't have to be in a state of false alarm and alert, worrying if someone will or will not hire me or fire me or kill me. Instead, my body is fooled and soothed into thinking that that person is Anna, and since Anna loves me, my body can just relax, because it knows that Anna and I will simply have the same outrageously rollicking good time that we always have had.

TURNING AN INTIMIDATING PERSON INTO SOMEONE ELSE

SO HOW DO I turn an intimidating, two-hundred-pound woman (or man) into my friend Anna, who's five foot nine and gorgeous? I use Sense Memory.

Let's say that I am at an audition and I feel intimidated by the casting agent in front of me. I'll imagine that Anna is sitting where the agent is sitting. Say the casting person's hair is brown. My challenge is to make her hair (or his hair) into Anna's hair.

I try and imagine the color of Anna's hair. I try to be specific. Is Anna's hair darker than the casting person's hair? Is it redder? Shorter? Longer? All these questions force my senses to remember Anna's hair as clearly as I can. So I can really see her hair in front of me. So my body and psyche really believe that Anna is there.

When I see the casting person's eyes, I try to imagine Anna's eyes there instead. Are Anna's eyes greener? Bluer? More almond shaped? Brighter?

Sometimes, this is hard work. Initially, it may be hard for you, too. But let's face it, it's better than being paralyzed with fear.

When Anna and I were at college together, she used to wear a certain blue coat. Except when it was really hot, I remember her wearing it all the time, including on certain nights when we snuck out of our dorm and had outrageous adventures. Come to think of it, the coat was pretty outrageous, too. It was a bright, bright blue, and in those days, we were both big, big girls, so it was a big, big, bright blue whale of a coat. I still smile when I think about it.

At the possibly terrifying audition, I imagine that the casting person that I'm scared of is wearing Anna's coat, which helps me to believe it's Anna. So my body relaxes and I am happy to be there.

My unspoken, part-conscious, part-unconscious monologue with the casting person might go something like this: "I see your face. Anna's is a little longer. And Anna's eyes are a little lighter than yours. Anna's hair is longer. I'm beginning to imagine that Anna is in front of me. I see her blue coat, and as soon as I see that big, blue, silly coat, somehow I remember her smell. It's not as though she smells bad or anything, it's just that she has a special smell, and I'm remembering it now. My body's remembering it now and is tricked into believing she's in front of me. So I think I'm with Anna, and I have a friend with me and I'm happy."

Now, I'm not hallucinating, nor am I trying to. I always know it's the casting person who's sitting in front of me, and not Anna. But when I substitute Anna for the casting person, I begin to behave as if I were with Anna, so I relax. My voice relaxes and gets deeper and I'm more likely to let my sense of humor come through and feel warmly toward the casting person. I actually get happy, because I tend to get happy when I'm around Anna.

And let's face it, this happy version of me is a lot more likely to win me a job, and make people think I'm the kind of person they'd like to work with, than a Jane who's rigid with fear and a "good little quiet little scared little girl." Not that there aren't times when it might well serve me to be a good little quiet little girl. Because there are some people who can only deal with people if they're very quiet and well behaved. Of course, I don't generally spend a lot of time with people like that. If I can help it.

ARACHNOPHOBIA

THE FIRST TIME I remember Substitution really working for me was at an interview for a movie called *Arachnophobia*.

Frank Marshall was going to direct, and he, along with two—not one—but two, casting directors, were interviewing me for the role of Edna Beachwood, the football coach's wife. At the beginning of the interview, I remember consciously putting my attention on them (instead of being self-conscious), and I felt I was doing all right.

Then the door opened, and in walked Kathleen Kennedy, who had worked closely with Steven Spielberg for many years and who had, with Spielberg, produced *E.T.*.

Now, at first glance, Kathleen was the kind of woman I was used to being intimidated by. Not only was she successful, and in a position to hire or fire me, but not a hair on her head appeared to be out of place. Growing up, I had what I thought of as hopelessly unmanageable hair. Plus, I was always scolded for it not being perfect. So for starters I felt "less than." And not only was she neat, she was chic.

Her clothes even looked new. I, myself, was low on money at the time, and would have loved, but felt I couldn't afford, new clothes. So her seemingly new clothes were particularly intimidating to me, and could easily have made me feel "not good enough." I mean, I wasn't wearing rags, but I was casually dressed. In jeans and a formless, comfortable sweater. Whereas even the crease in Kathleen's trousers seemed unattainably perfect, as if it fell so precisely perpendicular to the floor that you could draw an architectural blueprint from it. She looked like everything I thought I wanted to be, but was not.

Nevertheless, I took a deep breath and somehow I remembered to use Substitution. And I made her into Anna. I saw Anna's twinkle in her eye, and I felt my face relax and smile and be warm, and I greeted her as if she were my best friend. Anna. I was at ease, easy, and accessible. The kind of person you'd want as your friend—warm, open, full of fun. In other words, the way I was with Anna. And I remember being surprised by how warm Kathleen Kennedy suddenly seemed in return.

I was also, thanks to the Substitution, the kind of person with whom most people would want to work.

I got the job.

Later, I came to like Kathleen a lot for being who she, in fact, is: warm and smart and terrific—and I didn't have to pretend she was someone else. But for that initial scary meeting, substituting my best friend sure did the trick.

HOW *YOU* CAN USE PERSONALIZATION

- ❑ Who are you uncomfortable with, but still have to spend time with (hopefully not a lot)?
- ❑ Who's someone with whom you feel extremely comfortable and able to be yourself? Some people who have worked with me start out not feeling comfortable with anyone, so I suggest they use an animal here with which they may feel comfortable, their pet, or even an imaginary pet. For the purpose of this exercise, let's call this substituted entity your "best friend."
- ❑ Try and imagine your best friend in front of you. Let's say it's a woman:

- ➢ Can you hear her voice? Her laugh?
- ➢ What special detail do you notice about her appearance? Her eyebrows?
- ➢ Her hair? A bump on her nose? The whiteness of her teeth when she smiles?
- ➢ Can you feel her hand on your shoulder?
- ➢ Is there a special perfume that she wears?

- ❑ Now try recreating these sensory details using a real but different person in front of you. Let's say it's a man with whom you feel uncomfortable. To get your body to believe he's your best friend, instead of Mr. Intimidation, some of the following questions should be helpful:
  - ➢ Can you see your friend's hair where the man's hair is? How is the man's hair different or the same? How different is its texture or color?
  - ➢ How is his voice different or the same as the voice of your best friend? Is it higher? Lower? More resonant? Less nasal?
  - ➢ Keep trying to believe you are actually talking to your best friend. Try saying, "I see her." And see if you don't.

Remember, not every technique works for everybody. But if you can master the art of Substitution, situations that were once difficult for you to deal with might even turn out to be fun.

MARVIN AND HIS LANDLADY

MARVIN, A FORTY-TWO-YEAR-OLD copywriter, had a landlady who used to yell at him. A lot. And for no apparent reason.

Plus, she was critical and nasty. In fact, she was clearly crazy, but when Marvin first moved into her apartment building, she reminded him of his mother, and all he could do when she screamed at him was to get crazy himself, feel himself beginning to disintegrate, and want to die.

I pointed out that his landlady was not his mother, although she could, possibly, throw him out of the house. Marvin and I knew we needed to find a technique, fast, for him to use when she started in.

Could he use a Personalization? What if he changed her into someone else? What if he put a red clown's nose on her, and big red shoes, and imagined her with a big horn that she would occasionally squeeze and that would make an outrageous honking noise? A noise that was surely no more obnoxious than the sounds she made when she yelled at him.

The clown didn't do it for Marvin. But imagining his landlady to be some crazy bum on the street did. After all, how seriously could he take some drunken bum on the street yelling at him, someone he didn't know, someone who clearly didn't know *him*? As, in fact, his landlady did not.

Marvin remembered a man on Hollywood Boulevard who he *knew* was crazy, a man who wore four old suits at the same time and who occasionally repeated the same phrase over and over, without any apparent meaning: "Day of the fish. Day of the fish. Day of the fish."

I asked Marvin to imagine that his landlady was this guy. When she started yelling at him, Marvin would hear the voice of the man on the street yelling, "Day of the fish. Day of the fish." Soon Marvin found it hard to do anything but feel sorry for the woman who lived upstairs.

Eventually he moved to another apartment, but at least, while he was living with her as his landlady, she didn't get to him anymore.

10

• Imagination •

Richard Bolaslavsky, considered to be the cofather of modern acting along with Stanislavsky, wrote a wonderful book called *Acting, The First Six Lessons*, in which, he devotes a whole chapter to Imagination as one of the most important tools of an actor. And so will I.

IT WORKS FOR ACTORS, IT CAN WORK FOR YOU

Imagination is a talent that we all have, naturally, as children. It doesn't go away when we get older. Sometimes, if we've been taught to suppress it, it may seem to have disappeared, but we can wake it up again. Which is a good thing, because your imagination can transform a lot of potentially miserable situations into experiences you could actually enjoy.

If the word "imagination" scares you, think of it as daydreaming. And you know anybody can do that. You don't have to go into some deep state of meditation in order to daydream. Or to get in touch with your imagination.

Sometimes, an actor needs only his imagination to get him through a role, and then he can read a play, say *Hamlet,* and immediately understand the character he is meant to play.

Let's say it's Hamlet. Seemingly out of nowhere, the actor will understand, well, everything. The situation. The complexities of Hamlet's psyche. What it's like to be a prince living in fourteenth-century Denmark. Feeling ambivalent about taking an action as momentous as killing a king. And on and on.

Sometimes, the actor's Imagination just goes there and the actor suddenly understands his character, his situation, everything. Sometimes it's not that easy, but often, thank goodness, it is. And it can be the same for you.

Let your imagination go, and see what parts of your life you can improve with it. Add Sense Memory, Substitution, and Personalization, and you could very well find ways of enjoying any situation at all.

DAVID GOT NERVOUS

DAVID, A FORTY-YEAR-OLD financial planner, was very shy. He was nervous about talking in front of people and having them see him. So at the group therapy sessions that his therapist urged him to attend, David just froze right up.

I asked him to use his imagination to create a new, wonderful, and even fantastic version of his ordeal. David closed his eyes and tried to visualize the new scene. I asked him to come up with as many sensory realities as he could.

We started with his sense of hearing. I asked him, if he could have any music at all in the group therapy session of his imagination, what would it be. He said, "Every Breath You Take," by Sting. I asked him not only to hear the song, but also to imagine Sting in the room. He was smiling now, a sign we were on the right track.

We went on to taste. I asked him to imagine having his favorite meal at the session. Now he was really smiling. He imagined roast beef, potatoes, gravy, and string beans.

For dessert, he chose strawberry shortcake with extra whipped cream. I asked him to let his imagination run wild. I asked him to imagine everyone in the room eating, even playing with the food.

Okay, it was an infantile suggestion, but he got off on it. Remember, his task was to create as outrageous a fantasy as he could, in which he would be as alive and as turned on as possible. This would balance the unhappy and almost dead state he usually found himself in at the group. It didn't matter that his fantasy was unlikely to occur.

When David imagined Susan, a writer in his group who had always intimidated him, with whipped cream all over her blouse, he loosened up and began to relax.

Soon, in his imagination, David and the other group members were playing with the whipped cream and smushing it all over their bodies. Putting strawberries in various orifices, that sort of thing. David was laughing now.

Next, he chose to imagine everyone in the group naked. It wasn't a sexual thing for him. It just made the room feel more homey to him, I guess. Besides, with all the whipped cream that was going around, at least no one's clothes were getting dirty.

David's eyes were closed imagining the scene, but he was speaking aloud, telling me what the other group members were doing, who was dancing with whom, who was eating what and how. He imagined that everyone was telling him what they liked about him, and that he was telling them what he liked about them. He even imagined that he and Susan were dancing together.

He still saw himself in the group therapist's office, but he had changed its scenario, and he was having fun. He had all his favorite foods and toys, why wouldn't he have been having fun?

The group's therapist was a man with a beard, whom David initially saw as a fairly imposing figure, so we put some food in his beard. This seemed to make him more human and less intimidating.

I was not asking David to hallucinate any of this once he got to the group. But in a way, he'd been projecting warrior killers onto the group's members. This was a way to remove this projection, to change them from a punishing parental horde into just ordinary folks.

Two nights later, ten minutes before David went to the group, he replayed this scene in his mind, so he was relaxed when he went in. Later when he found himself tightening up, he would recreate one of his imaginary, sensory objects. The whipped cream in his therapist's beard seemed to work wonders.

Little by little, David opened up at the sessions and began to talk.

Is there any situation in *your* life that you need to rethink, loosen up, where you could have more fun? What imaginary foods, music, clothes, or games would make a situation fun for *you*? Yes, they're imaginary, but remember, if you're working sensorily, your body will actually believe all that food and music is there, and behave and react as if they really were there—so you will be having fun. Or at least your body will think you are. So at least the sweaty palms and frozen words will be gone. You have to admit, that's a start.

HOW ACTORS USE THEIR IMAGINATIONS

ACTORS ARE OF course trained to imagine things that aren't there.

In the movie *Save the Tiger,* Jack Lemmon plays an alcoholic. He drinks a lot of glasses of scotch in that movie. And you better believe that every glass he downs is not filled with real scotch. Not for forty takes in one afternoon. You bet it's colored water. He's only imagining it's something else. And he does it brilliantly.

In Chekhov's play *The Cherry Orchard,* Lyubov, the owner of the orchard, looks out into the audience and talks about the beautiful trees she sees in front of her. Just as Meryl Streep and Vanessa Redgrave have had to do. Of course, they will not see trees. In reality, all there will be in front of them is the back of the theater, an exit sign, and the faceless heads of the people in their seats.

The actress playing Lyubov must imagine those trees, whatever trees make her feel the way Lyubov is meant to feel when she looks out at her orchard: love, longing, sadness. An actress might imagine she was seeing some happy event of her childhood that makes her feel that way. Or she could imagine she was seeing trees.

When Superman flies through the sky on your television screen and points to a building below him, you bet there is no building below him. Just the floor of the room where he's been harnessed into his flying suit. The actor playing Superman has to imagine the building, or wherever it is he's going to save Lois Lane.

EXERCISES FOR YOUR IMAGINATION

IS THERE SOME situation you want to make easier?

What could you add to it (secretly) that would make you smile? Animals? Vegetables? Minerals? A favorite friend? What clothing could you imagine on either yourself or others that would relax you and make you grin?

VICKY USES A BEAR

VICKY WAS A forty-two-year-old graphic designer getting over a difficult divorce. She claimed to have come to me to learn how to flirt, but it soon became clear that she was lonely and she really wanted a friend. I soon discovered that there was no friend with whom she felt totally at ease, and whom she trusted.

I asked her to close her eyes and imagine herself with an imaginary best friend. First, I asked her to imagine herself somewhere physically, to describe the place sensorily, so she could access her unconscious more easily and come up with the deepest answers possible.

Vicky said she was sitting on a bench at a zoo. I asked her to describe the bench, the day, the trees around her. Finally, she imagined a woman sitting next to her on the bench, the "best friend" we were looking for. But when she and Vicky started talking, the woman turned out to be judgmental. This was not what we wanted.

I asked Vicky to let the woman go, and I asked for more sensory information on what she saw around her.

"In the cage ahead of me, there are bears," she said.

I asked her to describe one of the bears. She did. He was big and brown, warm and friendly. And nonjudgmental.

"Could *he* be your friend?" I asked.

The whole notion of having an invisible bear as a friend might have seemed slightly ridiculous to her, but she was, by nature, drawn to the slightly ridiculous and it amused her. She liked the idea of this bear being her friend, and she began to talk to him, in her imagination, and she began to smile.

When Vicky first came to me, she didn't enjoy going out alone. I suggested to her that when she went out for a walk or to the store she imagine the bear was with her. She said she would try.

I asked her if she could even imagine the bear giving her a warm kind of bear hug. She could. And it felt good.

Vicky started going out with her new friend. To the library. To the park. Somehow, even when she felt afraid, she felt he was there to protect her. As her parents never had been. Plus, she had someone to talk to, who would listen without judgment.

Vicky soon began to attract other friends. Not bears. Supportive, loving people. Thanks, I am sure, to her initial and wonderful relationship with her big, hairy, imaginary bear.

11

• Playing a Character •

ONE WAY TO transform who you are, how you feel, and how you behave, is to play a character. Just that. Play a character. Robin Hood. Marie Curie. Superman. The President. The First Lady.

Think of this exercise simply as fun. I am not asking you to believe you are Napoleon or Marie Antoinette. This is not an adventure in advanced schizophrenia. But by playing Napoleon, Marie Antoinette, or any other character that means something to you, you can bring out aspects of your personality that you feel need to be expanded.

Say you're going out on a date, and you wish you felt, and even were, more charming and debonair. You might try playing Cary Grant. By playing him, through the magical alchemy of acting, you may well find you suddenly allow yourself to be charming and debonair. Whereas, if you were simply "yourself," and that self had been taught to be serious, dull, puritanical, whatever, it might not be so easy.

If you're a woman and hunger for more adventure in your life, maybe you should try playing Amelia Earhart. If you wish you had more sex appeal and outrageous panache, you could try playing

Madonna. Cary Grant used to say, "When I wake up in the morning, I look in the mirror and wish that I were Cary Grant."

In a sense, Cary Grant had created an ultimately archetypal image of his personality, basically an image of charm and savoir-faire. This, in fact, is the image he came to project in his films. Many women associate sex appeal and outrageous panache with Madonna. For some, her image holds those projections. Of course, anyone could look in the mirror in the morning and feel ugly, stupid, or afraid, no matter what people had projected onto them.

For these exercises, the characters you will play will be mainly archetypal public projections. If you need a little dumb jerkiness in your life, if you tend to be too serious or intelligent, you could always try playing Goofy the Dog.

IT WORKS FOR ACTORS, IT CAN WORK FOR YOU

Playing a Character really can transform you. Robin Strasser, who starred in the soap opera *One Life to Live* for seven years on television, used to get fan mail saying, "When I need courage, I just pretend that I'm your character. And I find the courage."

WHY IT WORKS

WHEN YOU THINK you are playing another character, when you are concentrating on his or her characteristics, you not only forget your own limitations, but also allow parts of you to show that for whatever reasons, you have been afraid to let other people see. Which perhaps you have even been afraid to see yourself. Courage. Softness. Whatever. In a way, Playing a Character is just a trick. But every so often, it comes in real handy.

Some women I work with just have to think they are businessmen (that's right, *men*) and, automatically, their voices lower and become more authoritative. They talk more slowly. They feel more secure.

Yes, these women could analyze why they don't feel entitled to be strong and assertive. They could also do that until fish grow on trees. What I'm suggesting is a quick technique to get them acting the way they wish they could. This book is about giving you tools to take action. You may be surprised to see how your insides change as your behavior does.

I have nothing against analysis or therapy. They have given me some of the most thrilling lessons in my life. But there is a time for analysis. And a time for action.

HOW IT WORKS

IT IS NATURAL for us to imitate. Aside from being a kind of flattery, it is also a release.

If someone complains at you all day long, kvetch, kvetch, kvetch, you will come home at night and tell your wife or husband, or whomever, "Evie whined at me all day today. Kvetch, kvetch, kvetch." And you will imitate her easily, without even trying.

As naturally as we take in food or drink, we take in images, intonations, even other people's thought patterns. Some people can reproduce them more easily than others, of course. I happen to be one of them, although this is not always a good thing. Sometimes, if I'm talking with someone who's English, I start to speak with an English accent, which can be very embarrassing, since I'm not English. So, if you feel this is not your most accessible talent, don't worry about it. Just trust it's there inside you somewhere.

I mean, who can't imitate a baby? Just watch those supposed grown-ups goo-goo-gooing at babies, imitating, perfectly, the baby's inflections and movements. Perhaps because they are not threatened by the kid. Or because they think it's cute. Whatever the reason, they can do it. They *do* do it.

You can do it, too. I am asking you to *play*, as you probably did when you were a kid. Maybe you played a cowboy or an Indian. Maybe, even now, you can imitate Clark Gable playing Rhett Butler saying, "Frankly, Scarlett, I don't give a damn."

Playing a Character should be fun. If it is hard work, it probably won't be as effective as using another technique in this book. In which case, try another technique. Clinical studies have shown that children who watch tapes of courageous role models end up unconsciously modeling these characters. Children can do it, so can you.

NOW IT'S YOUR TURN TO PLAY A CHARACTER

- ❑ Choose anyone. Someone you like. Someone you don't. And just for the purpose of reading further, choose one now. Cary Grant. Britney Spears. Batman. Your favorite femme fatale. Anyone.
- ❑ How does your character stand? Does he lead with his head or his pelvis? Does he stick his neck out? Figuratively as well as literally? Is his body hunched or straight? Are his shoulders close to strangling him? How close? Is he tense? How tense?
- ❑ How does your character walk? Big steps? Small steps?
- ❑ What kind of clothing does he wear? Baggy? Tight-fitting? How does it effect how he stands and walks? Is he dressed stylishly? Vulgarly? Idiosyncratically? What colors does he wear? Are they muted? Bright? Mismatched? Always be as specific as possible.
- ❑ How would he hold his hands? In the air? At his sides? Relaxed? How relaxed?
- ❑ Is his smile open and wide, or are his lips pursed so you can hardly tell if he's smiling or not?
- ❑ You might try checking all of this out in front of a mirror. This makes it easier for some people.

- ❑ Maybe take a makeup pencil and change the shape of your eyebrows. How does that make you feel? What shape would your character's eyes be? With concentration, not to mention makeup, you can change the shape of your eyes. You can. You can give yourself an eyelift, if you just think of those eyelids lifting and see your eyes smiling instead of drooping. Visualization and all that. Yes, it takes time. But think about it, you know how your face changes depending on what you have been doing or thinking. It looks one way after making love and another after you have just paid the bills.
- ❑ Find a hat—if your character might wear a hat. How does it feel on your head? Do you notice how it changes how you walk, and your posture?

A hat, a walk, a perfume, any one detail may make you feel like the character and then you are home-free. Sometimes Sir Laurence Olivier needed only to find the right hat to wear for a character, and the walk, voice, speech patterns, even the psychology of the character he was to play, all fell into place.

Jack Lemmon said that for the movie *Missing* the flat brimmed hat he wore helped him feel more contained and even repressed. The hat "put a lid," as it were, on his usual expressiveness, and this helped him play his role.

Birdseed in my hair helped me to find Gloria, the pet shop owner in *Rocky*.

HOW I PLAYED THE PET SHOP OWNER IN *ROCKY*

AFTER I WAS cast for the role of Gloria in the movie *Rocky*, before working in front of the camera, I worked on the character with the director, John Avildsen. John wanted me to make her mean, so the audience would have extra sympathy for Adrian, played by Talia Shire, who worked for me in the pet shop. The script had me telling her to clean out the cat cages. John and I talked about other ways of making her mean, drawing the line at my throwing cigarette butts in the fish tank.

Finally, the day came to shoot. We were in South Philadelphia. In an actual pet shop. Cameras and lights were everywhere. We started to rehearse the scene. I said my first line, and you'd better believe I was mean.

Stallone stopped me. He wanted to speak to John. Privately. He wanted to know why I was so mean. They talked, and then John came over to me and said, "You gotta make her less mean." And I had two minutes before the cameras were supposed to roll to come up with another character.

For the life of me, I didn't know what to do. And then, call it what you will, inspiration or insanity, I put birdseed in my hair. Not a lot. But yes, birdseed. I saw it on the counter. I put it in my hair. And it changed everything.

It made me feel a little crazy. I started shaking my head (maybe to get out the birdseed, I'm not even sure). The shaking was barely visible, but suddenly, I felt like some weird pet shop owner named Gloria. I belonged in that shop. I was part of that shop. I knew how to relate to Rocky. I was the character. And everyone loved it. Even me.

So try anything. You can never tell what will work.

ROLES FOR YOU TO PLAY

LET'S SAY THERE'S a situation in which you want to try to play Marie Antoinette. Maybe because you are going somewhere and you feel that you won't be assertive enough, or that you'll be too nice and offer yourself up as a doormat. Ask yourself the following questions:

- ❑ How does she walk? Slowly? Quickly? Smoothly? Toe, heel, toe, heel? Heel, toe, heel, toe?
- ❑ How does she sound?

- ❑ What does she eat (what kind of cake)?
- ❑ How does she hold her neck? Her fork? Her eyelids? Any one answer could find her, and suddenly your whole body, your voice, even your speech and thought patterns could become hers.
- ❑ Now walk around the room as the character.
- ❑ And here is the trick: ask yourself what in your body feels different when you walk around as the character. This will serve as a trigger for you if you want to recreate the character later. Are your shoulders wider? Your heart higher? Remember the sensation: So if you need the moxie of, say, Alexander the Great in some boardroom, you'll be able to tell your body how to bring it back.

PLAYING JAMES BOND

BILLY, A THIRTY-YEAR-OLD computer analyst, dreaded going to parties. They made him freeze, he said. He couldn't talk, couldn't move. He showed no trace of the humor and the intelligence he obviously possessed.

A short, slight man, Billy decided that the character he wanted to work on was James Bond. Because, he said, he felt he wanted Bond's power and strength.

I asked him to walk around the room as Bond. I asked how it felt. He needed to walk around some more before he could answer.

"I feel wonderful," he said.

"Why?" I asked. "What feels different?"

"My muscles feel different," he said. "Taut, more alive."

I asked him to be more specific.

"There is a tingling sensation in them."

I asked him if he could give it a color.

He said it was red.

Who knows why his muscles felt red and tingling when he

thought he was James Bond, but they did. And they made him feel taller and stronger and even more powerful. And now all he has to do is remember that sensation, that red tingling in his muscles when he goes to parties, and he feels like James Bond, and this somehow gives him the license to talk, to feel free, and even to enjoy himself.

LEARNING TO PLAY THE PERSON WHO INTIMIDATES YOU

THIS IS A neat trick. If someone makes you uncomfortable, if someone seems intimidating, or somehow annoys you, play that person. Your discomfort, intimidation, or annoyance might disappear. By playing the feelings underneath a bully's bravado, you may come to understand his terror.

Try playing the saleslady who seems to look down her nose at you, who seems to look at you as if she thought you were a worthless piece of dirt. You may find that her body is really saying, "Of course, I hate you. I wish I had your money. I'm poor and feel like a worthless piece of dirt."

THE GLASSY-EYE SYNDROME

ROBERT WAS GOING out with a woman he really liked. Except when her eyes went kind of glassy. This annoyed him.

I had him play her, asked him how her body felt, asked him to imitate how she held herself, her head, her shoulders. I had him pretend that he had her glassy eyes. I asked him what he might be feeling if his own eyes were that glassy.

After a few minutes, he was imitating the way she opened her eyes a little wider than "normal." And once he approximated the distanced glaze in her eyes, it didn't take long for him to be able to speak out the thoughts and feelings that went with the posture.

"I have glassy eyes," he began.

"How do they feel? Try to be more specific," I said.

"I have glassy eyes," he said. "They are big and round and can hardly see. Because they are afraid of what they will see."

He realized that she felt afraid when her eyes went glassy. This realization made her more human for him, and he suddenly saw her with greater compassion and understanding. He felt it wouldn't bother him so much if he were with her and her eyes went glassy.

When I asked him how it felt to experience her eyes, he admitted he understood the feeling all too well. He realized that his own eyes occasionally went a little glassy (which I had noticed). He realized that, in fact, he was often afraid, himself. And he realized that he disliked his own fear, and that was why he had disliked hers. Not bad for just Playing a Character.

OTHER CHARACTERS YOU COULD PLAY

HERE ARE SOME of the characters people have played in my workshops. Maybe they will help you discover a new and special side of yourself, or inspire you to come up with others. Or they could just be fun to play.

- ❑ Winston Churchill—for strength and presence.
- ❑ Captain Kirk and Jean Luc Picard (from *Star Trek*)—for unflappability and courage. An amazingly large proportion of my students choose to play them.
- ❑ Madonna—for whatever she is selling at the moment.
- ❑ Goldie Hawn—playing Goldie somehow allows people (including me), to be lighter, more playful, and to have more fun.
- ❑ Jacqueline Kennedy—For power and elegance.
- ❑ John F. Kennedy—For power and elegance.
- ❑ Just for fun, you might try playing:

    Daffy Duck

- ❑ The Red Queen from *Alice in Wonderland,* (the one who's always screaming "Off with his head!")
- ❑ Ivan the Terrible
- ❑ Marilyn Monroe

Sometimes, I'll ask shy women to play brazen hussies, or cloddish brutes to play Fred Astaire. It helps to develop the buried sides of themselves, to balance them, and to loosen up an old self-image. On what new self-image do *you* want to focus?

CHRISTINA KARRAS

WHEN I SPOKE to the actress Christina Karras, she was preparing to shoot a film called *Second Advent*. She was playing the lead, and loved the role, because her character was strong, full of passion, uncompromising, and full of integrity.

"I can feel that part of me growing inside of me," Christina told me.

I asked her to be more specific.

"I feel that the character I'm playing wouldn't do anything that would stop her growth as a human being. Sometimes I, Christina, might sacrifice my own growth to please someone else. I've done that. I feel I'm less likely to do that since I've started working on the role."

Play a Character, and see how playing that character can influence *you*.

HOW ACTORS RESEARCH A CHARACTER

Some actors do research for their roles. For Alan Rudolph's film *Mrs. Parker and the Roundtable,* Jennifer Jason Leigh, who signed on to play the complicated Dorothy Parker, did her own extensive research.

She went to New York and checked into the Algonquin Hotel for a week, where Ms. Parker had spent so much time. There, she read everything the author had ever written, all her poems, short stories, and plays. She listened to recordings of Ms. Parker's voice. She filled an entire eleven-by-fifteen-inch notebook, six inches thick, with articles, photographs, and notes. She did this to digest as much as she could about her character, so she could feel her, in a sense, from the inside. She wanted to know Parker as well as possible to portray her as deeply as she could.

Sean Penn, preparing for his amazing portrayal as an autistic man in the movie *I Am Sam,* spent a lot of time with a man who was actually autistic to find out exactly how autistic people spoke, moved, and behaved.

So if you want to try playing Theodore Roosevelt, you could pick up a biography on him. If it's Daffy Duck you're working on, you could watch a cartoon. If you want to try playing Muhammad Ali, you could do what Will Smith did, and watch films of the boxer and train for four hours everyday. Or you could just let your character fill you up, and play that person from your intuition and let it fly.

RESEARCHING YOURSELF THE WAY AN ACTOR WOULD RESEARCH A CHARACTER

AND WHAT ABOUT when you play yourself? If you're not playing yourself as well as you wish you were, try doing some research. Maybe you could read some of your own early journals to figure out who you were before, which might help you figure out the best way for you to get where you want to go now. You might discover old patterns of behavior that you want to repeat, or some you might want to eliminate. By reviewing old accomplishments, you might see clearly what actions worked for you and which didn't, so you won't make the same mistakes twice. Or fifteen times.

You might research what your favorite friends have been like, and notice how and where you found them, so you can go and get some more, if it's more friends that you want. You could research what activities and dreams have made you feel good about yourself in the past, and think if any of these would be useful to you now.

Actors write down what their characters *want,* their characters' "objectives." They know not only what their characters want in every scene of a play or movie, but also what their characters want from their *lives*.

Try and do this for your own life. What do *you* want. Do you know what you want to do *today*? This week? Next month? What are *your* objectives? Do you have any one-year goals? Five-year goals? Ten-year goals?

Understanding where you want to go can help you figure out a way to get there. To get to Paris, first you'd have to know you wanted to go there. Then you could figure out how.

12

• Animal Exercises •

MARLON BRANDO STUDIED a gorilla as part of his preparation for playing Stanley Kowalski in *A Streetcar Named Desire*. He observed and imitated the gorilla's behavior and then incorporated parts of it into his performance. He watched how the animal stood, how he stared, how he moved, how he roared.

If you watch how Brando moves in that movie, and hear the sounds he makes, you can probably see the gorilla in his performance. If you're not looking for it, however, I don't think it's obvious.

But listen to the brute force of his bellowing "Stella!" Watch how his limbs seem heavy, lumbering, and alive in a way that sometimes only animals seem to be alive.

Brando worked for a time at the Actors Studio, where its founder, Lee Strasberg, would often have his actors crawling around on the floor as ducks, pigs, or elephants, anything they could think of that they felt could help them with a role.

Just as you can't tell that Brando was using a gorilla for *Streetcar,* or that Robert De Niro was using a crab in *Taxi Driver*, so no one is likely to know if *you* are using an animal for your life.

Try this exercise. You may experience some pretty amazing results.

HOW *YOU* CAN PLAY AN ANIMAL

YOU PLAY AN animal in much the same way that you play a character. You ask yourself many of the same questions and try to act the answers out with your body. Pick an animal and see if you can answer the following:

- ❑ If your body is your animal's body, how does it feel?
- ❑ Where is the animal more relaxed than you are?
- ❑ Where is it heavy?
- ❑ How does it move its mouth? Its ears? Its cheeks?
- ❑ How does it lie down, sit, crawl, walk, or roll over?
- ❑ What's it like to have a tail? Exaggerate this.
- ❑ How does it feel to have hair as long as your animal's? How long is it?
- ❑ Are its eyelids heavier or lighter than yours?
- ❑ What kind of sounds does your animal make? Dare to be outrageous here. Really trumpet that elephant, or let that lion roar. Really jabber that monkey. And when you hoot as that owl, can you feel its eyes, open and staring?

IT WORKS FOR ACTORS, IT CAN WORK FOR YOU

Playing an animal has liberated an amazing percentage of my clients. As one lawyer said to me, "It's strange, I feel self-conscious playing myself, but not when I'm playing a panther."

HOW ETHAN HAWKE USES ANIMALS

ETHAN HAWKE SAYS that one of the most important and effective techniques he uses is playing an animated cartoon animal. Yes, an animal from a cartoon. "When I get a role," he says, "I think what animal the character would be, because animals have character."

After he's decided what animal his character might be, he asks the same questions you'd ask in the non-cartoon Animal Exercise: Does the animal move quickly or slowly? What kind of sounds does it make?

I don't know what animal he was playing in *Training Day,* but he sure is brilliant in that movie.

Hawke has even said, "It's the most useful acting tool I know."

ELSA'S CAT AND HER TAIL

ELSA, A TWENTY-SIX-YEAR-OLD graphic designer, complained to me one day about the pain in her lower back. My cat, Chamomile, happened to be in the room with us and I noticed her rolling around on the floor in a particularly free and relaxed fashion.

Elsa always enjoyed watching Chamomile. She also had a cat, and loved cats, and something in me told me to ask Elsa to play the cat.

Elsa was game, and got down on the floor and tried to imitate how Chamomile was moving and breathing. I asked her to try and duplicate Chamomile's relaxation. It's hard to be much more relaxed than a cat.

Elsa began moving her nose the way a cat moves its nose, and her hands and arms, the way a cat moves its paws and legs. Most important, Elsa began moving her tail. Well, first, she pretended that she *had* a tail. Then she swished it around. She was even having fun.

**IT WORKS FOR ACTORS,
IT CAN WORK FOR YOU**

With all of the exercises in this book, I've found that if you're having fun, you're probably doing something right, and you'll usually get results.

Sure enough, as Elsa continued to move her imaginary tail from side to side and up and down, her lower back began to relax and the pain began to disappear.

I suggested she continue the exercise after she left me, walking to her car, or shopping at the mall. I suggested she could do it subtly, not that she get down on all fours and roll around on her back. She had only to remember how she had felt on my floor, as the cat, and to swing her hips, if only a little, as if there might be a tail at the end of her coccyx.

Elsa began to do this everywhere she went, and the best part is that the pain in her lower back disappeared.

Why? Well, as I mentioned in chapter 6 on Relaxation, images are the language of the body and our right brain. Images often translate themselves, almost immediately, into spontaneous, even unconscious behavior. Therefore our bodies usually react more quickly to being given an image than to being given a verbal command.

Enough analysis. Try imagining *you* have a tail if you want your back to relax and see if it relaxes the way Elsa's did.

DO YOU NEED TO SLOW DOWN?

SOME PEOPLE WHO work with me feel they rush too much. That is not surprising, considering that most of them live in the city and drive a car, which for starters goes faster than their own biorhythms. Then there's fast food, jet planes, instant net communication; you know the list.

Many people who come to me feel they go so fast they can't enjoy their lives. Often they find they can slow down by Playing an Animal.

Playing an elephant is guaranteed to slow you down. Rhinoceroses come in a close second, along with sloths and turtles, but it's elephants that are hard to forget.

ROBERT'S GORILLA

ROBERT, A THIRTY-TWO-YEAR-OLD coffee machine salesman, was used to being intimidated by the people he did business with on the phone. Yelling was apparently one of the ways they did business, and when they yelled at him, Robert would begin to shake inside, back down, and, as he said, "react." He would forget the position he had meant to take with them and what he had wanted to accomplish in the call. He said he wished he knew instead how to stand his ground.

In one workshop, Robert chose to work on playing a gorilla. Who knows why this animal gave him extra courage and a powerful sense of being, but it did. Standing as the gorilla, Robert found it easy to stand his ground. He sensed the gorilla would not be intimidated by anybody's yelling and might even occasionally roar back, even easily and effortlessly.

Robert and his gorilla man the phones together these days. They know where they stand. They do not back down.

BUILD YOUR OWN MENAGERIE

- ❑ What animal do you think would be fun for *you* to play?
- ❑ A puppy for playfulness?
- ❑ A swan for grace? Or a gazelle?
- ❑ A tiger or a puma for power and strength?
- ❑ An eagle to help you gain perspective on your life, to help you see an overview, to help you see the big picture?
- ❑ A butterfly?

At one workshop I gave at the Esalen Institute in Big Sur, everyone was playing an animal outside on a deck overlooking the Pacific Ocean, when I saw a butterfly passing by. A white and delicate, fluttering butterfly.

I tried to imagine how the butterfly would feel the wind. I imagined how intensely it would smell the flowers. I tried to imagine how intoxicated it might be from their smell. I felt a whole new appreciation for the nature around me, imagining I was a butterfly.

What could *you* learn from playing an animal, maybe a snake, or an orangutan?

Choose an animal and have a good time.

PARTY ANIMALS

IN THE FOLLOWING story I'm using the technique of Substitution (see chapter 8 on Substitution) but I've put this story here because an animal is being substituted for something else.

Vicky, an assistant costumer, had been going out with Joe for about six months, but she got nervous when she had to meet his friends. They were a little older than her, and many of them intimidated her because they were movie directors and producers.

One couple, in particular, made her uncomfortable. She told me about them, and it turned out that she knew some of their problems. They had both been playing around. Now they were in therapy together, to try and "work things out."

I pointed out that they were, like Vicky, human, imperfect, and in their own way, even wounded. For some reason, if Vicky imagined them as wounded deer (she felt a great affinity with deer), she felt at ease with them. She could imagine the freckles on their faces were the spots on a deer's body, and that their shoes were cloven hooves.

Many of us are less afraid of animals than we are of people. Of course, most of us don't live in the jungle, and we haven't been maimed by an elephant, or chased by a tiger. When we do see animals, they tend not to be threatening. They're cute little pets, or if they're wild, they're in cages, so we know we're safe.

IT WORKS FOR ACTORS, IT CAN WORK FOR YOU

Feeling safe is what these techniques are all about. It's from that safe place that we dare to be our true selves, as funny or as smart or as anything else as we can be.

Who are *you* afraid of? What animal could you turn that person into, so that you could be less scared? A rabbit? Your favorite puppy? A giraffe? This adjustment probably works best if the person you're changing is tall. Find out what works for you.

MY CAR, THE HORSE

IN THE FOLLOWING story I'm using Sense Memory, Substitution, and Imagination techniques, but I've put this story here because it's an animal that I'm substituting for something else.

I get tense, sometimes, driving my car. I like my car, but I learned to drive late in life, and there was even some sort of dictum in my family that women shouldn't drive. Driving was not ladylike enough, too aggressive, something like that. Yes, this could cramp a person's style, but that was in New York City, many years ago, and you really didn't need to drive a car there to get around.

But I live in Los Angeles now, and if you live in L.A., you really have to drive a car. A lot of the people I know live at least a half-hour away from me. Meetings can be an hour away. So I drive.

I know that lots of people have to drive. But most people don't seem to get tense when they drive. Usually, I do.

So what do I do? I imagine my car is a horse. Horses relax me.

Cars do not. Horses are breathing, living, alive, and exciting. Cars are metal, cold, and it seems pretty clear, potentially lethal.

So when I'm driving my white car, I imagine I'm riding a white horse, and my whole body relaxes, I find myself smiling, I sit up straight, pull my stomach in, and I start having fun. Driving becomes fun. I feel the same exhilaration I feel when I'm riding a horse.

Good old Sense Memory saves the day. Maybe I'll imagine *seeing* a white mane, *hearing* a whinny, or *smelling* some special smell. Maybe I'll *feel* the animal's haunches under me, and imagine that it's the horse that's making me bounce up and down. Somehow, if I feel the movement of a horse, instead of the movements of a car, I feel safe.

13

• Finding Your • Perfect Prop

PROPS, WHICH CAN be any objects at all, carry their own mystery, magic, and power. This chapter will show you how to find objects that somehow allow you, remind you, or inspire you to feel and behave however you want. Walk into a job interview with the right object in your pocket and it's possible that you'll feel so strong and terrific that you'll perform so brilliantly, the job will be yours. Arrive at that party with the Perfect Prop in your wallet and you just might have the time of your life.

Eleonora Duse used to carry an old, dirty piece of string in her pocket and would touch it every night before she went on stage. She said it "reminded her of her humble beginnings."

Who knows what memory the string evoked, or what strange event from her past this worn out piece of cord may have summoned up. Somehow, it gave her the courage and inspiration to go out on those stages and be brilliant and shine. When she performed in a tragedy, most of the audience was sobbing by the end of the evening. Somehow that little piece of string ignited her aliveness and allowed her to get in touch with her talent and power.

What object might make *you* feel most secure, relaxed, and loved? Or maybe you'd prefer to find a prop to help you feel silly? They're all out there.

AN EMMY AWARD-WINNING PROP

HERE'S A STORY about the actress Joanna Miles, from when she played opposite Katharine Hepburn in the television version of Tennessee Williams's *The Glass Menagerie*.

Joanna had a certain scene with Hepburn in which Joanna had to cry on cue. When Joanna and Hepburn rehearsed the scene, Joanna cried on cue. They shot the master (or long shot) of the scene, and again Joanna cried on cue. They shot the medium shot of the scene, and again Joanna cried on cue. When they shot Hepburn's close up, Joanna cried again.

When it came time for Joanna's close-up, the crew moved the furniture around so the cameras could get their shots. Suddenly, Joanna couldn't see the arm of a certain red couch, which she had been looking at during the other takes.

When they shot Joanna's close-up, and they got to the part where she had to cry on cue, Joanna couldn't cry. She was embarrassed, and felt even more like a fool thinking that the reason she couldn't cry was that she couldn't see the arm of that red couch. Somehow, that arm had given her something that had actually helped her emotionally enough to cry.

The director asked her to do the scene again. Joanna started the scene, got to the part where she was supposed to cry, and again she couldn't cry.

The director asked her what was wrong. Embarrassed, she told him she thought it was the fact that she couldn't see the arm of the couch. The director asked that the couch be put back in her line of vision, and the cameras rolled.

This time, Joanna cried. On cue. She saw that old, soft, somehow tender couch arm, and she could cry. Who knows why. Maybe her grandmother used to smooth her brow on a couch like that. Maybe the color of the couch was the same as her mother's dress when she kissed her good night on her fifth birthday. The bottom line, of course, is that she knew that couch arm was helping her, and she asked for that couch arm, got it, and it got her through the scene.

She knew the Perfect Prop that could help her and she's brilliant in that scene, and in that role, and more than deserved the Emmy Award she received for it.

WHAT PROPS CAN HELP *YOU*?

SET THE SCENES of your life with whatever props will get the best performance possible out of you.

- ❑ What if you carried a special handkerchief from someone you love?
- ❑ Or a special ring?
- ❑ Or a teddy bear (a small one in your pocket, not necessarily a big one in your lap)?
- ❑ Or your grandfather's pocket watch?
- ❑ In your office, could there be some special paperweight that might inspire you?
- ❑ What would a bowl of candy do for you—either on your desktop or in a drawer where no one else could see it?

IT WORKS FOR ACTORS, IT CAN WORK FOR YOU

If any of these objects work for you, or you know other objects that will, get them out there. Use them. Flaunt them. The key is to find something you connect with emotionally that will reassure you in tough situations.

A BANANA IN YOUR PURSE

HALLIE, THE FORTY-YEAR-OLD mother of a daughter with cerebral palsy, was having a lot of trouble dealing with meetings to find out what special education her child needed. Even admitting that her child was disabled was initially a difficult and even shameful experience for her.

Plus she found herself intimidated by the school directors, medical specialists, and educational experts she had to visit. Each new learning center seemed to present its own special ordeal.

And then she thought of putting a banana in her purse. That's right, folks. A banana in her purse. Not peeled, mind you. And not one she was going to eat so she could throw the peel on the floor and someone could slip on it and fall and she could laugh. It was just a regular old banana in its skin. In her purse.

Because somehow, that banana in her purse made her smile. Just smile. Inside. For some reason, that banana allowed her to see a certain ridiculous side of life, and suddenly her life didn't seem that serious, or her situation so dire, or the director or headmaster as intimidating as before.

She had a secret, a secret prop in her purse, which no one knew about but her, and suddenly, she felt relaxed and secure and as though she had a handle on life, or on the ridiculous aspect of it, and she felt just fine, and she went into those interviews with that banana in her purse, and those interviews were no longer horrendous for her.

So, is there some object you can put in your purse, or in your shoe, to cheer *you* up, to take the pressure off, and lighten things up, so you can enjoy your life?

Maybe it's your granny's locket in your pocket.

THE MAGIC STONE

USUALLY, IN THE middle of my workshops, after I've started people working on their Sense Memories, someone will ask something like, "How can you really talk to your boss and visualize a tree on the back of the boardroom at the same time?"

To illustrate that you can talk to anyone at all and simultaneously be aware of a sensory reality, like the tree or a dog or a stone, I started bringing a basket of stones to my workshops, stones that I happened to have picked up at the beach, although any stones will do; and I'd ask everyone to pick the stone that attracted them the most, the stone that "had their name on it."

Then I'd have everybody feel their stone in the palm of their hand, and say, "I can feel the stone in my hand and talk to you at the same time."

The second part of the exercise may sound a little airy-fairy-out-there, but the results have been so helpful, healing, and even self-revelatory, that I continue to use it.

I don't remember exactly how the second part evolved, but one day I just asked the class to continue holding their stones in the palm of their hand, in silence, and then I asked everyone if they could hear, or intuit, any words or message coming from the stone.

To my surprise and everyone else's, many people got answers. They had done the six-part preparation, they were centered, relaxed, and open, and miraculous as it may sound (even to me), practically everyone got some message.

No, I don't think stones talk. I do think that they can focus our energies and sufficiently center us so that we can hear whatever inner voices we may not otherwise be able to hear, maybe because we're running too fast to stop and listen, or we're too frazzled or off-balance. Or maybe because we're looking for answers from outside, instead of from within ourselves.

So, here's the second part of the exercise:

- ❑ Find a stone. Any stone. From anywhere. A stone that attracts you, or calls to you in some way.
- ❑ Then hold it tight in the palm of your hand. Either hand.
- ❑ Then see if you can get a message from the stone. A sentence, an image, advice, whatever comes up.

❑ If you got something bracing, inspiring, or something you need to remember like "Relax," "You're enough," or "Everything will be alright," carry that stone around in your pocket. Touch it when you need bolstering and it could be your Perfect Prop.

MYRNA'S MAGIC STONE

MYRNA, A TWENTY-NINE-YEAR-OLD caterer from Burbank who was feeling insecure about herself, got the words "You're enough."

I could have said those words to her for the next five years and who knows if she would have listened to me. But somehow, hearing them from a stone, *her* stone, ultimately from her own voice, she gave them more credence. She was amazed, not only because she wondered if she had actually heard words from a stone, but also because those were the exact words she realized she needed to hear, and in fact, had been longing to hear. So she heard them and began to believe them.

I had Myrna take her stone home. In fact, everybody who takes my workshop gets to take their stone home. I suggest they carry them around in their pockets, and touch them and listen to them when they need to, when they feel insecure, ungrounded, or nervous about any particular situation in which they find themselves, or into which they're headed.

Yes, there are thousands of people out there walking around with stones in their pockets. And now you may be one of them. The best part is, no one ever has to know that the stone is there.

Just put one of your hands into one of your pockets, just the way anybody might put a hand into one of his or her pockets. The only difference is, you'll feel your stone and hear its message.

People who have worked with me tell me this makes them feel centered and safe. They not only hear the message, but also feel a sense of belonging, both to nature and to the workshop they took. The stones seem to reconnect them to the solutions they discovered in the workshop, for getting over their self-consciousness, for feeling more themselves, for whatever. The bottom line is, they really work.

I myself have been known to pick up a stone on a nature walk, or at the beach, put it in my hand, and listen. Most often, it will tell me something I needed to hear but hadn't known how to discover. Here are four examples of what people have heard from their stones in my workshops:

"Love yourself."

"Don't settle for anything less than you need."

"You are eternal, like the ocean."

"Everything's going to be fine."

MARKS'S MAGIC STONE

AT A PRIVATE session, Mark, a twenty-eight-year-old dentist, picked up a stone, but he didn't hear any message from it.

I asked him why he had picked it.

All he could think of was that that stone, as opposed to the others, "had many colors."

In social situations, Mark did not feel he "had many colors." Instead, he felt invisible and had trouble speaking. Somehow, he would allow himself to get wiped out, perhaps obeying some distant parent who had told him to be seen and not heard, and who, Mark must have felt, really wanted him to be invisible as well as inaudible. For whatever reasons, Mark felt unworthy and invisible—in other words, without any colors at all.

I asked Mark to make a list of his own colors, to remind him that he was not invisible, but instead, present and alive. I had to pull some of them out of him (after all, he wasn't used to seeing or hearing himself), but we finally came up with the following list:

- ❑ Funny. (Mark had a sly and wonderful sense of humor.)
- ❑ Intelligent.

❏ Serious.
❏ Playful.
❏ Independent.
❏ Compassionate. (In our second session, he had developed a new compassion for himself as a little boy whose parents had yelled at him.)
❏ Dramatic. (I pointed out his long black hair, and how stylishly he dressed.)
❏ Shy. It was one of his colors, why not acknowledge it? Not necessarily as a liability, but as an interesting color that could, at times, even be attractive and self-revealing. Besides, I pointed out, shyness is a sign of a body protecting itself, a commendable trait—we need to protect ourselves from people until they prove themselves worthy of our trust. I explained his shyness could even be an asset, if it didn't prevent him from doing or saying things he really wanted to say or do.
❏ Willingness to change. (This was why he had come to me.)
❏ Courage.
❏ Fear.
❏ Appetite. Mark not only loved food, but he acknowledged he had a hunger for life.
❏ Perseverance. (Mark had finished dental school, even though, halfway through, he had gotten tired and bored and totally fed up with it. Still, he had finished, and he was proud of the fact. He acknowledged that he wouldn't have felt good about not finishing what he had begun.)

While Mark and I made the list, he held the stone in his hand. I suggested that when he was out in the world, and had those terrible moments of wondering who he was, and feeling invisible, that he had only to touch the stone and his list of "colors" would come back to him. He tried it, and they did.

By "anchoring" the memory of our lesson with the stone (one of the techniques of Neuro-linguistic Programing), Mark's physio-neurological system could replay the sensations of our lesson, the self-affirmation, the mirroring, the self-seeing. In our session, he had experienced being *seen,* and later, when he began to feel slightly out of control, he needed only to touch the stone to remember that he was, indeed, visible.

CYNTHIA'S MAGIC STONE

CYNTHIA, A TWENTY-EIGHT-YEAR-OLD clothing designer, had mixed feelings about living with her alcoholic boyfriend. When she went to the pile of stones I had put in the middle of the workshop floor, she picked up a big dark stone, held it in her hand, and listened. When it was her turn to tell the group what she had heard, she said she had heard nothing. Then, looking at the stone, she said, "You are too heavy and you drag me down, and I'm letting you go." Then she threw the stone across the room onto the floor and added, "Just like that."

The whole room, including Cynthia, realized that the words she had spoken were really directed at her alcoholic boyfriend. And when she spoke those words, she suddenly felt that there was a part of her that could actually say to her boyfriend, "If you drag me down, and are black and toxic, I'm letting you go. Just like that." She said she even felt that it might be as easy for her to let him go from her life as it had been for her to throw her stone across the room.

Maybe it wouldn't be that easy, but at least she suddenly had a sense that it was possible. She was tired of being dragged down by her boyfriend and his drinking, and now change seemed possible.

Pretty amazing for a simple exercise with a little stone.

14

• Finding Your • Perfect Costume

WEARING THE PERFECT costume can change how you walk, talk, think, and feel.

You know this from you own life. If you're wearing a dress that's too big, you may feel sloppy. Or you may feel safe because you feel hidden. If you're wearing trousers that are too big and they fall down, you may feel ridiculous. On the other hand, if you're wearing something that you're afraid doesn't fit right, you could also feel ridiculous. Or inept. Or "not together." And there goes self-esteem. There's no telling what effect a piece of clothing can have.

If you go to a party where you think everyone will be dressed casually and it turns out to be black tie, and you're wearing jeans, sneaks, and a T-shirt, you may even want to leave. On the other hand, this may be all you need to feel special and unique.

Find out how different clothes make *you* feel. Experiment. If you're used to wearing dark colors, see how you feel wearing brighter colors. You could start small, with a scarf or a shirt, and work up to a suit or a dress.

Find out what costume makes you feel fabulous. Then flaunt it.

Harrison Ford, so brilliant in so many movies, says, "Wardrobe is critical. Clothes are important because you move differently in different kinds of clothes, you feel differently in different kinds of clothes." For his role as Indiana Jones in *Raiders of the Lost Ark* he went with his costume designer to search for what would be exactly the right hat. Not only did it help him find his character, it never comes off in the movie.

According to the costume designer for *Oceans 11,* George Clooney and Brad Pitt took hours choosing the right costumes.

How would wearing different hats make *you* feel? And if you added a ribbon? Or a flower? Or three flowers?

Notice how adding even a little pin to your costume can change your whole mood or sense of yourself.

SUZIE GETS SEXY

SUZIE, A NINETEEN-YEAR-OLD college student, loved feeling sexy, and wanted to spend more time feeling sexy.

She realized that when she wore a plunging neckline with a push-up bra, she felt sexy.

So sometimes, even if she were wearing a turtleneck sweater, she imagined that she was wearing a low-cut blouse and push-up bra. And she felt sexy. As I explain in chapter 7 on Sense Memory, it doesn't matter whether you are actually wearing a blouse or sensorily recreating that blouse, your body will think that it's wearing that blouse.

PUTTING TOGETHER YOUR PERFECT COSTUME FOR THAT SPECIAL OCCASION

LET'S SAY YOU have a special occasion and you're not sure what to wear. Maybe it's your twenty-first-birthday party. Or your fiftieth. Maybe it's your boss' fiftieth birthday party. Maybe it's a special date. Whatever it is, here's an exercise that might help you find the Perfect Costume.

Sometimes, when an actor needs to figure out what to wear for a certain role, he'll close his eyes and imagine his character on a blank screen in front of him, and then let himself see, in detail, whatever his character may be wearing.

Try using this exercise for your own special occasion:

- ❑ Sitting in a chair, separate your ankles and drop your hands on your thighs.
- ❑ Close your eyes.
- ❑ Take three deep breaths.
- ❑ See a screen in front of you.
- ❑ Allow an image to appear on the screen: you in the Perfect Costume for that business meeting, or seminar, or costume party. Just let the image come to you. If it's for a business lunch, you might ask for your Best Business Self to appear and see what that self is wearing.

The trick here is to allow your unconscious to come up with whatever it invariably knows is the Perfect Costume. Let whatever comes to you come to you. You may learn something about yourself that you did not know.

AN EMMY AWARD-WINNING COSTUME

THE WONDERFUL AND versatile actress Dorothy Lyman credits her costume with helping her to understand and play the outrageous Opal Gardner on the soap opera *All My Children*, for which she won two Emmy Awards (one for every year she did the show).

Dorothy told me that when she first saw the script, she panicked. The role was written for someone much older than her, as well as for someone overweight, which Dorothy never was. Plus, unlike her character, Opal, Dorothy had always dressed conservatively.

Using an obviously fertile imagination, Dorothy "worked from the outside in," and tried to come up with what costume she could wear. You've heard the expression; "Clothing makes the man"? Well, Dorothy claims her costume made her character.

She went out and found what she called "f—— me pumps." They had spiked heels that made a slapping noise when she walked. They might well have shocked the pants off of her, except that she chose to wear very tight spandex pants. Then she added a wig, "teased real big," and went out and bought a lot of costume jewelry, full of fruit and fish, with no one piece costing her more than a dollar ninety-nine.

Then she looked in the mirror. She wasn't seeing Dorothy anymore, but instead, a character vastly different from herself, someone with so much conviction, that in a sense, she convinced Dorothy that they were one and the same person.

Dorothy even believes that playing Opal ended up changing her own personality. Before doing the role, Dorothy says she had been insecure and unsure of herself. Opal was not afraid of anyone or anything, and was far more assertive than Dorothy had ever been. When Opal first appeared on the show, she had only seventy cents in her pocket. When she left, she not only owned her own business, but was running for public office. Still wearing the spandex pants and fruit earrings.

Dorothy's own career went on to include not only acting, but also writing, directing, and running her own theater.

There's no telling what could happen to you if you slap on a few baubles and a pair of shoes.

FINDING THE RIGHT MAKEUP

MAKEUP IS AS much a part of the Perfect Costume as anything else you might put on your body or head. I believe I'm mainly talking to women here. But, whoever you are, here's my advice. Experiment.

Try different shades of rouge and lipstick. More strident reds.

Softer pinks. Try different shades of eyeliner and mascara. How would blue on your lashes make you feel? Use anything for inspiration. Models in magazines. Paintings from the Louvre.

Natasha Richardson, in preparing the title role for the Broadway production of Eugene O'Neill's *Anna Christie*, used Edvard Munch's painting *The Scream* as the model for her makeup. Now you know why her Anna had wild red fever spots on her cheeks, with purple shadows, and unevenly painted, garishly bright lips. Although that makeup is probably not the one you're looking for.

ELLEN MAKES HERSELF GLAMOROUS

ELLEN, A FORTY-SIX-YEAR-OLD history professor, felt she didn't know how to make herself look or feel sexy or glamorous. She was right. I sent her to one of those makeover artists who tell you what colors you look best in, and what kind of makeup to wear. She had never used dark liner around her eyes, or color on her lids. She had never worn bright lipstick. She had never worn *makeup*.

Ellen hardly recognized herself after her session. But she loved what she saw. And somehow the image she saw in the mirror gave her the freedom to feel and act sexy and glamorous.

Plus, Ellen looked wonderful.

15

• The Magic "As If" •

CHILDREN KNOW HOW to Act As If they're whatever they think they want to be. Cowboys and Indians, Pochahontas, whoever. Somehow, their imagination just takes them there.

Acting As If is not as superficial an exercise as it may at first seem. A good actor is led along a secret, even invisible path, and suddenly he feels As If he were Hamlet, Picasso, or Pochahontas, just as the audience sees him as if he were Hamlet, Picasso, or Pochahontas. Acting As If requires a trust from the actor that he will be okay if he lets go and in many ways becomes someone else.

Trust and letting go are not easy for some people. Particularly for people who feel tense in social situations, and therefore do not trust their "audiences" not to hurt them, or themselves to let go and be however they are without fear of retribution.

Let's say you decide to Act As If you were a lion. Well, you may start roaring and feel stupid, but it's also possible, if you really let go, that you will feel the essence or archetypal energy of Lion enter you, and you will know, understand, and even feel that you are a lion. It is a kind of state of grace. If your image is strong enough for you (for you, mind you, not for anyone else), your ability to trust, just let go, and surrender to the image will take you there.

It's what happened when I pretended that someone had leprosy (see *introduction*). I just acted As If he had leprosy and, almost magically, I kept away from a man who was otherwise dangerous for my health. Who knows or even cares why leprosy worked for me, and scarlet fever might not have. I've never known anyone who was a leper. But I guess I've read and heard enough about leprosy to have something stored in my memory cells, and my body reacted automatically.

My imagination took over, which is one of the cornerstones of any acting performance, and happens when an actor is truly acting As If he were the character he's meant to be playing.

There are degrees, of course, to which it occurs. An actor playing Henry V can Act As If he's in a palace, sitting on a throne, but usually the actor knows, at least on some level, it's just a chair from the shop with some extra red velvet on it. Still, when the actor sits on it, As If it's a throne, he'll sit on it in a particular way, and it may make him feel important, or in awe, or *something* special.

I'm going to show you how to give your unconscious a conscious order to Act As If—the way an actor acts as if he were a prince, if he's playing Hamlet. The way any actor in the musical *The Secret Garden* will Act As If he were in a real garden, even though he's on a stage surrounded by a lot of plastic plants and flowers.

What we're trying to do here is correct what we could consider an unconsciously mandated and negative "as if." The way nervousness, when you're giving a speech, makes you act "as if" there were lions out in the audience instead of normal humans, or "as if" the person interviewing you for a job might, at any time, hold a knife to your throat. And that's when you have to program a positive "as if," and Act As If the audience were made up of your favorite dolphins, or As If the interviewer were your best friend. Or maybe you could just Act As If another person, whom you totally loved, had his arms around you and were kissing you all over. Sense Memory sometimes kicks in unconsciously, so that without consciously asking to hear your best friend's laugh or see twenty dolphins leaping above the waves, you might simply hear the laugh or see those mammals.

What we're really talking about here is a suspension of belief. The same suspension of belief you have when you go to see *Hamlet* and you know you're not in Denmark, and that even though Hamlet is murdered on stage, at the end of the play, that the actor playing Hamlet isn't really dead. Somehow, you've started believing in the circumstances of the play, and there's no risk in this "fooling yourself," there's even pleasure. You even know, instinctively, that if it's a good play, you could have a good time, or even a catharsis, if you allowed yourself to believe as real what you know really isn't real, and so you do.

A lot of the exercises in this book can bring you to that state of suspended belief, and then you just start believing in whatever As If you've chosen at the time.

If you're doing a Sense Memory of a waterfall, it's so that your body will begin to Act As If it were there. You may, at first, have to work hard, sensorily, to get the Sense Memory to work for you. Ultimately, however, you may only need to tell yourself to Act As If you were by that waterfall, and your senses will buy it, and your breathing, your relaxation, your emotional state, and even your speech will change.

IT WORKS FOR ACTORS, IT CAN WORK FOR YOU

All you may need to tell yourself is to Act As If you were Meryl Streep or Martin Luther King or Luke Skywalker, and your breathing, relaxation, how you walk, talk, even your stature, vision, and self-confidence can change.

HENRY'S SECRET GARDEN

HENRY, A THIRTY-YEAR-OLD owner of his own shoe manufacturing company, was fine when he had to sell shoes, but he froze at parties.

I asked him to try, when he was at one of these parties, to Act As If he were in his garden instead. I wasn't asking him to hallucinate, only to work on a few Sense Memories so that his body would *believe* he was in his garden, and begin to relax as if it were there.

Henry really loved his garden. He had planted all its bushes and flowers and vegetables himself, artistically and with care, and everything about the garden made him feel not only good, but also proud.

We worked on a lot of sensory objects for him to recreate so he could more easily and quickly believe he was in that garden. Dirt under his fingers. The smell of cucumbers, tomatoes, strawberries.

Finally, by recalling a certain birdsong, he was there in a second. He had found a trigger, and all he had to do was hear that song, and all the sensory details of his garden flooded him without his having to work at them. Because his body, of course, knows exactly what it's like to be in that garden. That's the magic of the magic As If. Sometimes all you need is one little trigger, and, like Henry, you're home free.

In his garden, Henry felt whole and complete—unlike how he initially felt going to parties. He had seen parties only as somewhere he had to go in order to meet a woman because he was single and didn't really feel whole without a woman in his life. Suddenly he did feel whole at parties, because he brought with him the fullness he felt in his garden, tricked his body into relaxing, and significantly diminished his old desperation to find a woman to make him feel complete. It certainly made him a lot more attractive to women. And at least parties stopped being the torture they had been.

PAM GETS A LIFE

PAM, A FORTY-TWO-YEAR-OLD singer/songwriter, felt she was stuck in an accounting job because she didn't have the self-esteem to get her songs out to the public.

One day, she simply decided she was going to Act As If she had self-esteem. She hadn't felt as though she had any and in fact, few of her actions showed she had any, since she hated her day job and didn't feel she deserved a better one, and she felt so shy and genuinely unworthy of performing her songs in public that she had even stopped singing at clubs when they had an open mike night.

Pam started Acting As If she were a person who had self-esteem. Before making decisions, she would ask herself, "Would a person who had self-esteem do this?" Intellectually she knew what a person who had self-esteem would or would not do. She began, in a sense, by playing the playwright to her actress self.

The words "acting as if" seemed to work magic on her, and I was impressed, thrilled, and even a little amazed by the actions she began to take.

Pam went out and bought herself what she called "a snazzy outfit," a short skirt, a top with sequins, a pair of leather boots, and a pair of what she considered outrageously long earrings, which she loved, all of which she figured she would buy if she had self-esteem. Even though she doubted she was a person who had self-esteem, she acted As If she were, and bought it all anyway.

She got carried away by her role, that of A Person Who Has Self-Esteem. She knew that a singer who had self-esteem would go back to doing open mikes. So she started going to clubs and singing.

Her final test came at one of the open mikes when someone from a small radio station asked her how she would feel about performing on his show.

Her instinct was to say "Terrified. Good-bye."

But she had been Acting As If she had self-esteem for long enough now that she caught herself, and said, "Sure."

She was so proud of herself for saying yes, that her pride got her to the radio station and through her songs, which she actually sang well.

I saw her the day after she performed on the show. She was excited and glowing and still proud of herself. She not only liked, but even loved herself for having taken this uncustomary action.

Not only is Pam beginning to feel better about herself, but she is actually beginning to have some self-esteem. Maybe not as much as she will have next month or next year, but just for today, she's enjoying being who she is, and is more and more doing—and capable of doing—what she loves to do. Not bad for simply Acting As If.

This technique works wonders with some people. Maybe it will work for *you*.

· More Tricks · of the Trade

PART THREE

The eleven *techniques I describe in this section are subtler and may seem more mysterious than those in Part Two. Still, you will find that any one of them has the potential to turn around a situation that's fraught with difficulty and make it into an event that you may actually enjoy.*

The notion of being charismatic, for example, may be subtle, but knowing you're shining can make a big difference to your performance. You will also read about hearing music in your head and speaking the truth. You will learn a technique I have enigmatically named "The Inner Walnut." All three techniques can produce surefire and powerful results.

Have fun with your new bag of tricks. Honor them and they will serve you well.

16

• Using the • Psycho-Physical Action

Constantine Stanislavsky, (father of naturalistic acting), having initially concluded that Relaxation was the key to mastering the craft of acting, ended his life believing that instead the key was the Psycho-Physical Action.

Here's how Stanislavsky finally worked with his actors on a script. He had them break down every scene into "beats," or separate units, and for each beat, or even for every line, as well as for every scene, and even for the whole play, he asked his actors what their specific "actions," or objectives were.

He told his actors to label each action with an active verb, to make the action even more active, so that it would involve their bodies. Verbs like "to draw out," "to take a stand," "to connect" were used. Many actors analyze the scenes in their movies or plays by breaking them down into actions. Stella Adler and Robert Lewis emphasized Actions when they taught. Adler's students included Marlon Brando and Robert De Niro, Lewis's included Anne Bancroft and Meryl Streep.

Hamlet's Psycho-Physical Action (or objective) may differ depending on which actor is playing the role. One actor may decide Hamlet's action, for the play as a whole (his "super objective"), is "to uncover the truth." Another actor may decide his action is "to take revenge."

Actors playing Romeo and Juliet may decide their overall Psycho-Physical Action is to "express their love."

Was Sylvester Stallone's Rocky trying "to win," or "to go the distance"?

All these actions can, and inevitably do, have a physical component. Hamlet, wanting "to revenge his father's death," may express this action, physically, with a dagger. Romeo and Juliet may "express their love" by touching or kissing. Rocky's whole body will, obviously, "fight," in order to try to win in the ring.

The trick is always to come up with a verb that inspires your body to move. Once your muscles take over, your psyche will follow along with your desires, your feelings, and your soul. Your goal is to perform the action with your whole self. Thus the name "the Psycho-Physical Action."

Each verb will be inspired by what you *want,* based on what you *feel*. So say you *feel* hungry. And you *want* food. How will you get it? What will you try to *do*? Hunt? Beg? Cook? Go to a restaurant? Notice these are all verbs that you can feel yourself trying to accomplish both physically and psychologically.

So how can you use this technique in your life?

For that pitch meeting, do you want "to convince" the network that your program lineup should be used? Think how your presentation would change if, instead, you went in there "to stand up for yourself." Or "to save the world."

Think of any situation you're anxious about and try to think about what your action (or super objective) might be. Are you going to that party "to have a good time," or "to make a splash"? Do you want "to charm" your host, or "mother" him? Choosing the right verb can help your body to expedite your action and even help to make your wish come true. Now, how's that for feeling your power?

IT WORKS FOR ACTORS, IT CAN WORK FOR YOU

Defining the Actions in our own lives can only help us, because ultimately, it is our actions that define our lives and make us who we are.

AN ACTOR IN *BEVERLY HILLS COP*

THERE'S A SCENE IN the movie *Beverly Hills Cop* that always makes me laugh. It takes place in the dining room of a very exclusive men's club. The place is so stuffy the maitre d' is practically wearing a tuxedo. In fact, the actor playing the maitre d', a wonderful actor named Jack Heller, is wearing an extremely well fitted and appropriately conservative suit, with every unobtrusive hair in place.

Then Eddie Murphy comes in, wearing sneakers, jeans, and a sweatshirt and asks if a certain Mr. Maitlin is there.

Now you know that Jack's maitre d' knows that this African-American man in sweats does not belong in his exclusive club, and that no one in the club even wants to think about, let alone see, anyone even resembling Eddie Murphy's character anywhere near it. So when Murphy tells him he wants to go into the dining room and deliver a message to Maitlin, Jack asks if he can't deliver it for him.

And then Murphy, perfectly straight, well, actually, pretending to be outrageously gay, primps out something like, "You'd better tell him I have herpes simplex number thirteen and he'd better see a doctor or his you-know-what is likely to fall off."

That moment is funny enough, but I'll never forget Jack's reaction, and the look on his face when he says, "Perhaps you'd better tell him yourself." He's hysterically funny because he's so real there, and his performance so seamless.

I asked Jack what Action he had chosen to play.

He said, "To hide how shocked I was. To keep up a good front. To maintain decorum at all costs."

It's a perfect example of an actor choosing a simple action, and executing it simply and wonderfully. Jack's face is funny and wonderful, and truly his character's. The audience always roars. Because Jack is not thinking about his face, he's playing his Action. His whole body and mind and emotions and spirit are all doing their best "to keep up a good front." So all of him just *is* that maitre d'. Because Jack knows what he's there to *do*. He's there "to keep up a good front." And does he ever.

MICHAEL MAKES IT TO THE STUDIO

MICHAEL MADE STUNT suits for actors in movies. Forty-two and severely social-phobic, he found it almost impossible to talk to people he didn't know. He worked with a partner who could talk to their customers while Michael would concentrate on making the flying suits, jerk vests, crash pads, and harnesses.

One day, one of the movie stars for whom they had made a harness couldn't come to the shop for his fitting. Michael's partner was out of town. Michael would have to go on the set. Alone. And he was panicking.

Michael called me and asked what I thought he should do. He was afraid that everyone on the set would be looking at him, laughing at him, judging him. Such is the painful, absurd, and paranoid nature of social phobia, which, to some degree, most people experience at least once in their lifetime.

Michael was scared he would have to interact with people on the set, socialize, and be witty. These were expectations his father had of him when he was a little boy, but which were surely irrelevant to the task at hand. He only needed to fit the harness he had made so the actor could jump off the building and not die.

I suggested to Michael that his Psycho-Physical Action for the scene he was about to play might be simply "to fit the suit." Michael would then have not only an action, but also a silent Inner Mantra (see Chapter 21), which he could repeat in his head. "I'm only here to fit the suit. I'm only here to fit the suit."

I told him to focus on his Action, and only on his Action, when he got to the set: "I'm only here to fit the suit. I'm only here to fit the suit." This was to be his focus, not who might be looking at him, not what he imagined people might be thinking about him, not his exaggerated sense of inadequacy, but only the task at hand.

He had a task, he knew what his task was, and all he had to do was go on that movie set and do it. He was there to fit the suit.

Michael was amazed that his visit to the set went smoothly and without the panic and discomfort he usually suffered. A one-pointed focus does tend to make life easier.

Dr. Jeffrey M. Schwartz, a psychiatrist at the UCLA School of Medicine, explains in his book *Brain Lock* how people's concentrated focus on a task can actually help them to balance their brain chemistry.

So what Psycho-Physical Actions could *you* use in *your* life? At parties, maybe you could think you were there just "to have fun." Asking for a raise, maybe you could think you were there "to present your truth."

17

• The Meaningful • Pause

I'VE MENTIONED THIS theatrical trick before, but its usefulness and benefits are so great, I think it deserves a chapter of its own.

Lest you doubt that pausing looks "normal," watch a film, any film, and watch your favorite actors take their Meaningful Pauses. See if those times don't get and hold your attention at least as much, if not more than when they are talking.

Watch Al Pacino in *Scent of a Woman,* for which he won an Academy Award. Watch that final monologue in the courtroom and enjoy the pauses he takes. For emphasis. For dramatic effect. To collect his thoughts. To assess the temperature of the room. Or for who even knows why. The point is, every time he takes a pause, see if the audience doesn't pay even more attention—both the audience in that courtroom, and the audience in your theater.

Watch Ingrid Bergman and Humphrey Bogart in *Casablanca,* and see if the moments when they pause, and think or feel, aren't at least as moving as when they say any of their famous lines. After all, what would "Play it again, Sam" be worth, if you were cheated of the pained look on Bogey's face, both before he utters those famous words and after.

IT WORKS FOR ACTORS, IT CAN WORK FOR YOU

In this case: as in art, so in life. So look around you, see who pauses, and watch if when they do, people don't lean in a little closer to pay attention.

DARE TO TAKE A PAUSE

WHEN YOU'RE GIVING a presentation, or even in the middle of a story you may be telling at lunch, dare to be quiet for a moment. Watch your own audience grow even more silent than before you paused. Try it, just as an experiment.

Dare to Take a Pause. The ceiling will not fall down on your head. People will not laugh at you or point at you and scream "What is wrong with that person? Why is he so slow?" They will not throw stones at you, or take up a petition to have you deported.

When we fear such reactions we are probably dealing with feelings that we learned as children. Maybe it was from some evening at dinner, or some class at school, when we couldn't come up with an answer fast enough, and were punished for it, sent away from the table, or in some other way made to feel slow, stupid, or scared. So some of us learned to fear for our lives if we didn't come up with the right answer—fast.

But *now* if we Take a Pause, we have to remember that we are no longer that same helpless child and we have to stop acting as if we were.

IT WORKS FOR ACTORS, IT CAN WORK FOR YOU

Whenever you find yourself feeling more nervous than feels comfortable, dare to Take a Pause, and in that pause, summon up any technique from this book that you think might help you the most, and use it: A Sense Memory, an Inner Mantra, Three Deep Breaths, a Magic Stone in your pocket.

In that Pause, you could imagine you're smelling your favorite flowers, or ask yourself where you're tense and breathe into those places. You could hear your favorite song inside your head. If you like peaches, you could imagine you were eating one. I happen to like those white Babcocks. Every time I imagine I'm eating one, my mouth immediately relaxes and I start to smile. Experiment. It could even be fun.

Remember, your audience won't know *what* you're doing in those pauses. It's doubtful that anyone will even wonder. People might think you're simply breathing. And breathing has yet to be made illegal.

People will not necessarily think you're stupid. They might even think that you're "deep"—still water runs deep, and all that. Or they might think that you're thinking. That's always impressive.

DARE TO DO NOTHING

THE ULTIMATE CHALLENGE for an actor is simply to feel and *be* his character.

This involves "not doing."

Every other technique I talk about in this book involves some doing. Here, I'm talking about doing nothing, and just being.

Of course, if you *could* just be, in public, you probably wouldn't need this book. You could just go off and be yourself and have a totally terrific time.

This trick of "being" is so ultimately core to just being yourself in public that I'm devoting a whole section to it.

Maybe all the talking and performing we do in life is just an intermission in the middle of our "being," instead of the other way around. Either way, "being" is a really important talent to develop, and, if you're really lucky, you may even master it.

"Being" can be its own reward. There's a kind of surrender involved, a giving in to the moment, a trusting that however you are at any given moment is enough and okay and even terrific, a way of saying "Accept me as I am, or the hell with you. This is what you get, and it's good enough," spoken as a simple truth, without anger.

Many people study meditation to learn how to get to a place where they can just do nothing, think nothing, and where they can feel nothing but themselves, and their essence, or the force of a greater life essence, with which they feel at one.

This "being" is an ineffable state. It's a letting go and an owning at the same time. Sex gets some people there. Or nature. Or yoga. Get there however you can, but try to get there, to feel what, potentially, is a state of grace and bliss.

This is a section about stillness, about daring to be quiet. This is not easy, especially for people in the United States where doing and achieving have always been the ultimate goals.

Sir Anthony Hopkins remembers Katharine Hepburn telling him, when they first worked together in *A Lion in Winter,* that when the camera was on him, he should "do nothing." He had thought that acting was about "chewing up the furniture."

Hopkins says this was the most important and difficult lesson he had to learn as an actor. And just watch him use it. He's breathtaking in his stillness, not to mention terrifying, in his Academy Award-winning role in *The Silence of the Lambs*.

Or watch Ben Kingsley in his Academy Award performance as Gandhi. Kingsley says, "Silence and stillness are my two major currencies."

Often, the moments that impress us most are those where the

actor merely *is*. Bette Davis had a genius for it. Watch her in *The Little Foxes*.

When you understand how just to be, the Meaningful Pause will be easier to accomplish.

IT WORKS FOR ACTORS, IT CAN WORK FOR YOU

It takes a lot of courage simply to be still. Many people need to learn that if they're not talking all the time or telling jokes, that no one is judging them as not being enough.

Our society does not encourage us simply to be still. Nor is this something we are taught. We're not trained to feel our feelings, so very often the act of merely being is terrifying, because feelings could come up, and if we're not used to them, they could be scary. Or even painful. (If you think you need to be more in touch with your feelings, see chapter 3 on Emotional Preparation.)

I love that in the Old Testament the holiest day of the year is considered to be the Sabbath, a day when everyone is meant, simply, to be. Not do, not work, not even handle money, no less earn it, but simply be. The Sabbath is understood as a day of rest, the way God, presumably, rested on the seventh day after creating the world.

The Sabbath, the Bible says, comes at sunset like a bride, and one is meant to marry this bride whether one is a man or a woman. Which is another way of saying one becomes married to God—or light, or truth. Or wholeness.

The sense of being I'm talking about is synonymous with wholeness, which is what we all want to feel when we show up at an interview or a party, or let's face it, anywhere at all.

So, just for a second, dare to cease the work, and simply be. Be with yourself. Even at the party or business meeting. So the people who are deciding whether or not to do business with you or go out on a date with you not only understand what you are saying, but are also given a chance to feel a sense of your being. That's pretty exciting. And pretty impressive.

LEARN HOW SIMPLY TO BE QUIET

People speak of "observing" the Sabbath. One way to achieve this state of being is truly to *observe*—in other words, to be conscious of what's around you, of how your body is, what you're feeling, what you're hearing, or even the fact that you *can* hear.

I'm suggesting you try *just being,* as often as you can—maybe once a day for starters, then even for a moment every twenty minutes. Definitely try using it every so often when you're giving a presentation—to give your audience time to breathe, to let you have time to feel your fullness, your aliveness, in all its astoundingly complicated and miraculous simplicity.

I'm not asking you, suddenly, in the middle of a speech, to be quiet for half an hour, or to take an hour before answering someone's question.

I'm not asking you to veg out like an idiot and stare glassy-eyed into someone's face, until he or she screams, "What's wrong with you? Hello?! Are you there? Is anybody home? Are you alive?"

I'm asking you to take a moment to dare to relax, to let go of tension, to relax into that part of yourself that is always relaxed, so you can see better, and be better seen. So you can think better.

IT WORKS FOR ACTORS, IT CAN WORK FOR YOU

Try being still for a moment—so you can be more present, not only for yourself, but also for others. I'm asking you not to judge these silences, but to revel in them.

Try being part of a conversation and from time to time feeling comfortable simply being quiet. I'm not saying you have to sit there and never say anything, but surely you might judge a person who talks incessantly more harshly than a person, who, for whatever reason, simply chooses to be.

MOLLY GOES TO A PARTY

MOLLY, A TWENTY-SIX-YEAR-OLD dress designer, had a terrible time at parties because of what she assumed people were thinking about her if she wasn't talking. She thought she always had to be buzzing around the room, meeting people, making conversation. She thought that if she were quiet, it would be an admittance of failure, and proof that she was unpopular and a social disaster. She assumed the whole room would think this too.

I suggested she go to a party and try being quiet anyway. She was already having a terrible time buzzing around the room, how much worse could it be if she were still?

The first time Molly sat down alone at a party, and just breathed, she was very scared.

Then she told herself, "It's all right, I won't die. I'm just experimenting. It's safe to be quiet."

She took Three Deep Breaths.

She looked around. She took another Three Deep Breaths.

Then she saw a man across the room watching her. He was clearly interested. Another man was coming up to her from the other side of the room, about to introduce himself.

Molly was beginning to learn there can be payoffs for being quiet and still.

18

• Do You Have • Charisma?

WHAT IS CHARISMA?

Why is it that some people walk into a room and everybody turns around? Why do some actors shine and others not? And how can *you* produce and give off more light.

First, you must take up all the space you were meant to take up, be as big as you can be, both in your body and in your mind, so your energy can flow, so your light can come shining through, so nothing is blocked, not your talent, not your freedom of expression, not your intelligence, your voice, or your feelings.

After chiropractic adjustments, which expand the spaces in between the vertebrae and in the joints, photographs of people's electromagnetic fields show greater light around their bodies than before.

You can give yourself these expanded spaces and this extra light. One way is to breathe shining white light into the spaces between your vertebrae, as I suggested for your Physical Preparation. If you consciously breathe in light, any color light, your body will absorb it, register it, and then emit it. (For which we thank the laws of Sense Memory.)

And you will shine.

Another way is simply to love yourself as exorbitantly as you can. You know how people shine who are in love. Feeling safe and loved will also get you to shine. We expect lovers to be beaming. (A little sex doesn't seem to hurt either, and there's always a *little* love in there, isn't there? . . .)

If you're not in love right now, don't worry. There are techniques you can learn to feel the same euphoria. How else could actors play Romeo and Juliet convincingly? After all, actors don't fall in love with their co-actors on every single job.

Here's one technique to get you there. Think of a time when you *were* in love. Remember an exact moment of excitement or passion or romance and recreate it sensorily. In other words, use all five senses as described in the section on Sense Memory. Maybe it was a peak experience. Maybe it was when someone special said he or she wanted to marry you. Maybe someone simply touched your hand for the first time, and you've never forgotten the thrill of that moment.

If you find that dredging up old love affairs depresses you, imagine the *next* great love of your life. Imagine how the two of you will meet, or declare your love, or make love, and create *that* moment sensorily. Your body will believe it's happening and it will shine.

KNOWING THE RIGHT MOMENT FOR YOU TO SHINE

WHEN PEOPLE HAVE charisma, they walk into a room with all parts present—physical, mental, emotional, spiritual—and they're exploding with the full light of who they are. Literally, like a star. So that they're holding nothing back, feeling it's safe, *knowing* it's safe, to express everything and anything. The same way great actors know that it's safe to let it all out, on screen or on stage.

For some actors, sometimes it's safer to shine *on* stage or *on* screen than *off*. I'm always hearing about someone who's seen some well-known actor in a supermarket and thought, "Boy, doesn't he look awful," or "Wow, she looks dull." Whereas on screen, these actors are luminous.

Why? Probably because the actors haven't done any preparation to go into that supermarket and shine, the way they do before they act. Sometimes, that preparation is only their flipping an inner switch that tells them it's safe now to be all they can be.

Maybe when they were kids and screamed and cried, their parents scolded them or hit them. That was in life. But on a stage, they know it's safe to scream and cry. They even get applause. They even get paid.

IT WORKS FOR ACTORS, IT CAN WORK FOR YOU

You can do the same preparation that actors do when *you* want to shine. Look through Part One and see which techniques work best for you. The right preparation can turn your entire energy around, give you permission to let out your light, and know it's safe to be all you can be.

We are all born shining into the world. Sometimes people from our past have temporarily snuffed out our light. Many grown-ups are threatened by the life energy exploding out of their children. They don't know how to deal with it, often because they were forced to dim their own light because it threatened *their* parents. Dimming your light can become a bad habit if not checked. But it's also a habit that can be broken.

Incest survivors are sometimes the most dramatic examples of people who were scared into not letting themselves shine. As innocent children (we were all of us innocent, shining children), their bodies somehow assumed that they were molested *because* they were shining. Now they need to know it's safe to shine again, that no one's going to hurt them or molest them just for being who they are and shining.

IT WORKS FOR ACTORS, IT CAN WORK FOR YOU

We all need to realize that as grown-ups, we get to choose when and if we want to shine and when and if we want to stop ourselves from being all we can be. Sometimes, it isn't safe or smart; it can be inappropriate and even unkind.

Society has always been threatened by the spontaneous exuberant, the person who may suddenly and simply start singing and dancing in the street. Okay, it's probably a good thing that everyone isn't singing and dancing in the streets whenever they want. We'd have chaos. Not to mention a lot of noise, which is why there are laws that prohibit it (usually from ten in the evening until seven in the morning, because, yes, people need sleep and quiet time).

I'm not saying you have to dance and sing and scream in order to shine. You can be quiet and shine. But if you feel you want to shout and dance, and you don't, or worse, you want to, but you don't know you want to, you'll lose your shine and start to look dull. Look at the people around you and see if this isn't true. The most important thing here is to recognize whose voice it is that we're hearing when we choose not to shout or shine.

Sometimes Inner Mantras (or affirmations) can help here. You could repeat "It's safe to shine," or "It's safe to let it all hang out," or "It's fun to let it all hang out," aloud when no one can hear you, or silently in your head. Or you could write one of these mantras down on a piece of paper and carry it with you somewhere you want to shine.

Is there an Inner Mantra or even a poem that might work for you? For an interview with James Lipton on Bravo's *Inside the Actor's Studio,* Debra Winger wrote the first lines of "The Journey," a poem by Mary Oliver, on her hand. The poem, she explained to Mr. Lipton, helped her to stay centered, focused, and inspired. And so she was.

YOU CAN SHINE LIKE A STAR

WHAT DOES IT mean to be a star, except to shine? Everybody has what it takes to shine, not only Broadway and movie stars. Don't forget our very cell matter can be traced back to ancient star matter, which fell to earth and evolved into our DNA.

IT WORKS FOR ACTORS, IT CAN WORK FOR YOU

Our cells have in them the memory of shining, much the way an acorn has within it the knowledge of the oak tree it can become, and from which it came. That wholeness, that shining, that magnificence, is all in there. All we have to do is allow it to be.

HOLY RITUALS OF TRANSFORMATION

Think of the halos of saints and holy men. Not only is prayer another way to get in touch with your light, any ritual can get you there. Remember, actors were originally priests and holy men. Theater began in the temple. In ancient Greece, healing was also performed in the temple. For many actors, acting is still a holy rite, a ritual of healing, transformation, magic, and honor.

I first experienced this consciously when I started performing *Dear Nobody,* the one-woman play I performed for a year in New York and ended up playing on and off for twenty years all over the United States and England.

In my dressing room, every night before I went on, I felt I was putting on my costumes as if I were a priestess preparing to go before her congregation. In a sense, my goals were the same as those of a priestess. I was dressing to transform myself, and I hoped the words and feelings I would communicate would transform and uplift as much of my audience as possible, would make them feel better, or love more deeply, or look more deeply into themselves.

And when *you* want to shine, aren't you, also, on a journey of transformation? Sometimes, we need to transform ourselves from our Sleepy, Lazy, or Dull Self (all roles that have there place) into our Shining, Persuasive, Seductive Self to sell a product, attract a mate, or convince someone to hire us.

WHY DOES A BRIDE GLOW?

WHAT DOES A bride have in common with an actor on stage that shines?

The bride glows because, like the actor, she's feeling loved, special, and beautiful. She too has done her preparation—planning the wedding, choosing her costume (her wedding dress), finding her props (something old, something new, something borrowed, something blue). She too has a script ("I, Petula Brown, do take thee, Raymond Chandler, to be my, etc.").

Both the bride and the actor are in the business of transforming themselves. The bride, from a single lady into a married woman, (usually with a new name), the actor from, let us say, Mel Gibson into Hamlet. At best, both the bride's witnesses and Gibson's audience experience some sort of transformation and exultation as well.

IT WORKS FOR ACTORS, IT CAN WORK FOR YOU

You can analyze any scene you have to play as a ritual of transformation. Just know the transformation you are trying to make. All the techniques in this book are techniques of self-transformation, which is, after all, the art of the actor.

How do *you* want to change?

- ❑ From self-conscious to self-confident? See Chapter 26 on Self-Consciousness.
- ❑ From vocally monotonous to vocally exciting? See Chapter 22 on Improving Your Voice.
- ❑ From listless to sexy? See Chapter 29 on Feeling Sexy and Gorgeous.

IMAGINING APPLAUSE TO MAKE YOU SHINE

NOTICE THAT AFTER both a wedding ceremony and a play, for both the bride and the actor, there is applause. Applause has a sound and an energy you can easily recreate, sensorily, in order to feel inspired, supported, loved, acknowledged, accepted, and validated. In other words, applause makes you feel like a star.

Dawn Steele, the first woman to become a president of a major American motion picture company, Columbia Studios, says that before an important meeting, she'll imagine applause as she enters the room. That's right, she'll do a Sense Memory of applause. She'll hear it and feel its vibration, and you better believe she starts to shine.

Some people get scared at the sound or thought of strangers clapping for them. If you think that's true for you, go on to the next exercise. Other people just eat that applause right up. If that might be you, sensorily recreate that applause, with as many sensory details as you can.

- ❑ Try and hear the precise sound of the applause, its pitch, its timbre.
- ❑ Can you sense its rhythms, its loudness?
- ❑ Does it crescendo?
- ❑ How robust is it? Does it fill the whole room?
- ❑ Can you feel it in all the cells of your body?

For your big presentation you could even imagine that the business associates at your big meeting are your best friends, and it's your birthday and they've just sung "Happy Birthday" to you, and you've blown out your candles, and they're applauding, so you'll hear the song in your head, as well as the applause.

If this combination of sense memories works for you, you may well be feeling and showing the same glow as that bride. It's the same glow that lovers show when they're in love.

THE GLOW OF LOVERS

A SENSE MEMORY of making love also has the power to make you shine, and even make you look as glowing as you might if you had in fact just made love. Try it. Remember to recreate, sensorily, the other person's touch, smell and voice, as well as your own.

The lovers' ritual is not that different from the actor's or bride's or yours, if you're hearing that applause.

There's usually a script, maybe a few "I love you's." Then there's some kind of choreography or direction. Maybe the lover underneath gets on top. And there's usually some form of applause, someone saying, "You were great," or "Was it as good for you as it was for me?"

Yes, we all prefer the real thing, but in its absence you may be surprised by the glow you achieve, and by how good you look and feel, simply by doing the Sense Memory.

19

• Breathing Can • Save Your Life

I TALK A lot about Breathing in my classes. People tend to forget how important breathing can be. And how healing and centering. Breath is Nature's tranquilizer. When in doubt, take a breath.

Why? What does the oxygen do for you?

Here's a clue. When people with symptoms of senility are given oxygen, the symptoms very often disappear. SENILITY? Yes. Because the brain's fuel is oxygen. The magic and power of oxygen stimulates the brain so that logical thought is restored and can be communicated.

Ever get nervous or tense and wonder where your power of speech disappeared to, not to mention your ability to think? Did you ever think you could have performed better when you didn't? And you even wanted to hit yourself because you thought of the perfect response only after you had spoken another? An oxygenated, quick-moving brain might very well have helped.

**IT WORKS FOR ACTORS,
IT CAN WORK FOR YOU**

One of your body's responses to danger, real or imagined, is to hold its breath, which stops the oxygen from going to your brain—and there goes your usual power of speech and ability to think. Conscious breathing is the perfect antidote for people who get scared and hold their breath.

Dr. Andrew Weil has a wonderful book on breathing in which he explains the physiological mechanics of oxygen's ability to control our nervous system and therefore our anxiety. Experiments with Biofeedback come to the same conclusion. You probably will too.

TWO QUICK BREATHING TECHNIQUES FOR COUNTERACTING YOUR NERVOUSNESS

As I EXPLAINED in Part One, it's always a good rule to breathe from deep in your abdomen, expanding not only your belly, but also, ideally, your back and the spaces between your ribs. You get the most oxygen that way.

Actors know that if they need to be upset or even cry, shallow breathing will take them there. You're probably not reading this book to increase your anxiety or nervousness. But this makes my point: the more shallow and quick your breaths are, the more upset you'll get.

**IT WORKS FOR ACTORS,
IT CAN WORK FOR YOU**

The more deeply and slowly you breathe, the calmer you'll get—which is, of course, the state you want to be in for that important presentation or meeting.

So breathe as slowly, deeply, and calmly as you can, particularly if you start feeling nervous.

The following two techniques are ancient yoga teachings. Yogis have known for thousands of years that by breathing according to specific techniques, we can quiet the mind, calm our emotions, heal our body, and uplift our spirit. If I feel any panic before an audition or on a set, I'll do one or the other. Sometimes, both. Actually, if you go on a movie set or backstage in a theater, you can usually find an actor doing at least one of them.

ALTERNATE NOSTRIL CALMING BREATH

Alternate nostril breathing can usually center you and calm you down pretty quickly. It balances the sympathetic and parasympathetic nervous systems, just in case you've got a case of "nerves" before that presentation.

- ❑ Sit down—ideally in a cross-legged position. Doing this simply sitting in a chair will also do.
- ❑ Leave your left hand open on your left knee.
- ❑ Bring your right hand up to your nose, your right thumb closing your right nostril, your second and third fingers folded onto the palm of your hand, and your fourth and fifth fingers against your left nostril.
- ❑ Hold your right thumb tightly against your right nostril, so you can't breathe through it.
- ❑ Breathe out your left nostril. Let all the air in your body out of that left nostril.
- ❑ Now, breathe in through the left nostril, a deep breath, all the way from your abdomen, expanding your chest, back, and ribs.
- ❑ Hold both nostrils closed for a moment.
- ❑ Let the breath out of the right nostril, holding your left nostril closed with your fourth and fifth fingers.

- ❑ Breathe in your right nostril (still holding your fingers against your left nostril).
- ❑ Close your right nostril with your right thumb, holding both nostrils closed for a moment.
- ❑ Breathe out your left nostril, keeping your right nostril closed.
- ❑ Repeat the whole exercise, beginning by breathing in through the left nostril. Repeat four of five times, or as often as you want.

I'm always amazed by how even two rounds make me feel refreshed, clearheaded, centered, and relaxed. You can play around with how long you hold the breath and how long you take to let it out. For example: in three, hold three, out three. Or: in five, hold ten, out ten.

HOW TO TAKE AN ENERGIZING BREATH

WHEN YOUR ENERGY is low and you need to get it up, the following technique always seems to work wonders.

- ❑ Sit in a cross-legged position, or any way or anywhere that works, in your room, in your car, in a bathroom stall.
- ❑ Blow air out your mouth, as if you were blowing out a big candle that won't blow out.
- ❑ Repeat. Maybe five times. Maybe twenty. Play around with this. You can also do this by breathing sharply out your nose, as if you were blowing your nose into a handkerchief (which isn't there).

These sharp exhalations will work your abdomen, which is the energy source of your body.

The wonderful actress Tracy Brooks Swope says she won't go to an audition or onto a set without doing her version of this energizing breath.

Tracy exhales five times, then inhales for the count of five. She repeats this three times. She did this when she shot *The Big Picture* and when she shot *The Power of One*.

Tracy says this helps her to clear herself, so any and all emotions, as well as her talent, are available to her. "That way I'm free to let the work come through me. The breathing leaves the body free of anxiety and balances you like a Xanax, with none of the side effects."

TAKE THREE DEEP BREATHS

Over two thousand years ago, Taoist tradition taught that if things in your life were not going well, you were supposed to stop and take Three Deep Breaths, maybe because the Taoists believed that by breathing in, you could breathe in divine energy.

I think it is interesting that the word *inspiration* comes from the Latin word *inspirare* meaning "to breathe in." So, if you're looking for inspiration, for an important presentation or any situation at all, I suggest you try "breathing in" Three Deep Breaths.

I once had dinner with a psychologist for some of the big league baseball teams, the Dodgers and the Mets, teams like that. He told me that what he told the teams all came down to one big secret.

Say it's the World Series and the bases are loaded and this guy has to pitch. He's a little nervous, right?

So guess what this super shrink tells our American baseball heroes.

"Take three deep breaths." That's it.

"Take three deep breaths."

And for this, he's paid thousands of dollars.

More important, his teams do well.

Breath centers you. It brings you back into your body, a body that you could leave if you were scared and didn't want to be wherever you were. But a breath can bring you home to yourself.

So, for those moments of fear and trembling, when you can't think what to say, or you freeze, or your throat goes dry, TAKE THREE DEEP BREATHS. Your audience will probably think you're taking a Meaningful Pause (see Chapter 17 on The Meaningful Pause).

IT WORKS FOR ACTORS, IT CAN WORK FOR YOU

Don't be afraid of being quiet for those Three Deep Breaths. Many people believe still water runs deep.

ANOTHER ACTOR ON BREATHING

ACTORS GET NERVOUS, too. One of the best things an actor can do when he gets nervous, or finds he's not acting well, is to stop and take Three Deep Breaths. Or one or two. Then he has a moment to think about how he's feeling, or where he's tense, or what he should be focused on in that moment.

Michael Glicksman, the actor and songwriter, often uses breathing as a conscious technique. Before saying a line in a play, he told me, he'll take a deep breath, and "just let the breath itself dictate how the line will come out. Breath has an intelligence of its own, and when the actor surrenders to that intelligence he is so rooted in his body and its intelligence that the actor and the lines automatically become very real, centered, moving, and intelligent."

Michael told me he also uses breath to get deeply in touch with his feelings, and break through any blocks he might have. He'll take a really deep breath into some part of his body that feels tight, and by breathing into it again and again, he'll release both the muscle tension and the feeling that's been blocked there.

And before he sings any of those long lyric lines that he's written, to make sure he's not only perfectly heard, but also centered and full of feeling, he'll take Three Deep Breaths.

A DOCTOR ON BREATHING

STEPHEN, A FORTY-TWO-YEAR-OLD doctor of internal medicine, came to me because of how scared he got when he had to give presentations at his hospital. I told him to take Three Deep Breaths whenever he started to feel himself freeze.

"I'll look stupid," he said.

"Your inner kid will think *he* looks stupid," I said. I explained that some of us, as children, felt we had to come up with the "right answer fast," or die. That was what we felt then, because it was usually our parents who wanted that answer *fast*. Our lives depended on them, so if they were angry and withdrew their love and care, we *could* have died.

It took some talking to Stephen to convince him he wasn't going to die if he paused to take those Three Deep Breaths. It turned out that Stephen's parents had been extremely demanding. He remembered one particular occasion when his father had yelled at him for not coming up with an answer quickly enough, and Stephen had burst into tears.

I asked him to try to *see* himself as he had been as a little boy, scared and sure he had to answer on a dime or die. I asked him to see this little boy sitting to his left, and to say, "It's okay, Stevie, you can take your time. You're safe now."

This was hard for him, painful even, because of all the times he hadn't heard those words as a child. But he did it anyway.

I then suggested that he could speak to his imaginary young self, silently, at those presentations that had made him so nervous, during the pauses where he took those deep breaths.

Yes, this is an acting technique. Actors are constantly talking to people who aren't there. They look out into a dark theater, and though it looks as if they are talking to their best friend, usually their best friend is not out there, and they are only imagining that they're seeing their friend.

It also happens that on a movie set, an actor who *seems* to be doing a scene with the famous star of the movie will, instead, be saying his lines to an assistant prop manager, and the actor has to imagine that he is talking to the star. Some stars are just too busy or tired or self-centered or selfish to stick around for the other guy's close-up.

Yes, this sounds terrible. This *is* terrible. On the other hand, if an actor has to play a scene with some busy, tired, self-centered, selfish star, he may just want to imagine he's talking to somebody else anyway. (And he'll use Personalization.)

Stephen knows now that, at his presentations, when he takes those Three Deep Breaths (or even one or two), no one will know whether he's panicking, using one of the acting techniques in this book, thinking, or telling his inner little boy self, "It's okay Stevie, you can take your time. You're safe now." Anybody could assume he was thinking: "Yes, that's a very intelligent point I just made. I hope you got it, so you can follow me. Because the next one is a whopper."

It was a revelation to Stephen to imagine this, or that his audience could be thinking or feeling, perhaps even unconsciously, "Thank goodness he slowed down for a minute, so I can digest the last four points he made. Oh, how nice. I can breathe now, just breathe. Here's a moment when I can just take in that oxygen that keeps my body centered, happy, and logical, when it might otherwise go stupid, senile, and sad."

20

• The Power of Music •

WE ALL KNOW that hearing a piece of music can change our mood, or the state of relaxation of our muscles. Even plants respond differently depending on what kind of music is played to them. Plants seem to thrive more on Bach than on rock and roll. What about you?

Brain imaging studies have shown how music can "light up" the parts of the brain responsible for emotion and deep feelings.

Imagining music in your head is, of course, another form of Sense Memory. By giving a conscious command to yourself to *hear* something, you can get to your unconscious and transform your entire psycho-physical being.

So if somebody suddenly makes you feel uptight, even if you have no idea of what unconscious tape has begun to play in your head to make you uptight, remember that by giving your ears the right music that, let's say, makes you feel happy (the actual or the imagined music), your unconscious will start to hear a tape that makes you happy and your body will react as if the actual stimulus were there.

Imagine loud heavy metal music blaring in your ears. Some of you may be flinching. In which case, loud heavy metal is not what you want to tell yourself to hear when you want to feel and appear calm, centered, unruffled, and "together."

When I want to feel happy, I just hear a certain piano piece in my head (Chopin's Etude in E Minor) and I start to smile. I don't even know why. I just know it works.

What song, or what symphony, could turn everything around for *you*?

- ❑ A love song?
- ❑ A Mozart quartet?
- ❑ Drumming?
- ❑ Your favorite lullaby?
- ❑ A favorite Beatles song?

Not everyone is as affected by sound as by sight or by touch, but if you're one of the people who is, and if the prospect of a certain meeting is making you tense or anxious, hear that music in your head, before or during that meeting, and watch your body relax and your anxiety disappear.

SALLY KIRKLAND AND SAMUEL L. JACKSON

BEFORE SHOOTING HER amazing five-minute monologue in the movie *Anna,* for which she won a well-deserved Academy Award nomination, the wonderful actress Sally Kirkland listened to Bob Dylan's *O Mercy* album.

O Mercy is an album she likes to think she, in part, inspired, since she was dating Dylan when he wrote it. "I like to think friends inspire each other's art," she told me.

Right up to the moment when she had to go out on that soundstage to shoot the scene, she was in her dressing room listening to the album on headphones. "The songs," she says, "summon up tears of joy, pain, and compassion."

Watch her in that monologue, describing what it was like to be in a Russian prison and lose her husband and child. The camera never leaves her face once, and her performance is riveting. It's beautifully acted and a perfect example of the power of music both as a preparation and an inspiration.

Samuel L. Jackson, who received an Oscar nomination for his role in *Pulp Fiction,* also understands how useful it can be to perform and simultaneously hear music in your head, though no one else knows you're hearing it. In *Star Wars Episode II, Attack of the Clones,* playing the head of the Jedi Council, he imagined the movie's theme music in his head for his big fight scene. His energy and bravado in that scene are palpable.

LEARNING TO FEEL SAFE AFTER BEING RAPED

BECKY WAS A twenty-year-old woman studying to be a massage therapist. She had been molested as a child and ended up getting raped as an adult. What she wanted more than anything else was to feel safe in the world. Becky had learned martial arts techniques so she could defend herself if anyone should threaten her. She had been to therapy. But she still didn't feel safe in a way that mattered.

In the workshop she attended, we talked about her using Mantras, or Sense Memories of all kinds of security blankets, but nothing felt strong enough.

One afternoon, I asked everyone in the workshop to choose a character to play that they felt might help them in their life.

Becky tried to think of a character. Finally, she said, "I know what would make me feel safe. If I had a guardian angel. I'll play a guardian angel."

I asked everyone to stand up and walk around the room as their character, paying attention to how their character would walk, talk, move, and behave.

Becky started walking around the room as she imagined her guardian angel might walk. She found herself going up to other people in the room and gently, even sweetly, smoothing their foreheads. She said comforting, loving, supportive things to them.

Then, suddenly, she started singing, "Nothing's Gonna Harm You, Not While I'm Around," the lullaby from Stephen Sondheim's musical *Sweeney Todd*. Becky had heard Streisand's recording of this amazing song and loved it.

Becky began singing the song to people in the room, but she still found some sense of her own safety was missing.

Then she happened to wander into the hallway outside the workshop room and saw a mirror on the wall. She looked into her own eyes, and had the brilliant impulse of singing the song to the frightened face she saw in the mirror.

"Nothing's gonna harm you, not while I'm around."

Suddenly she felt taken care of, as if the words were coming from some deep well inside of herself, from some archetypal mother or guardian angel who had entered her and now sang to her and who she could always count on to be there.

It was the music, in addition to the words, that reached Becky's unconscious and allowed her to change how she felt. And now, simply by hearing the first lines of the song in her head, mirror or no mirror, she understands that she's singing it to herself and she feels safe and newly secure.

Thank you, Mr. Sondheim.

TEMPO RHYTHM

Sometimes actors can figure out how to play a scene by figuring out what is called its "tempo rhythm." In other words, its tempo (fast or slow), and its rhythm (even or erratic).

Sometimes actors can figure out how to move, talk, or even think as their characters by sensing the tempo rhythm of their character.

Try hearing a Strauss waltz in your head and feel how you change, or a Beatles ballad, or something you choose yourself.

Feel the music in your body. Can you feel your heartbeat change with its tempo rhythm? What if you heard it before you had to give a speech? Would you feel jollier? Smarter? More "up"?

IT WORKS FOR ACTORS, IT CAN WORK FOR YOU

Notice how simply hearing the music in your head changes not only how you feel, but also how you walk and move. What music gives more bounce to *your* walk? What music makes you walk assertively? The "1812 Overture"? A bossa nova? A tango?

How do you want to feel before you give that major presentation? Probably not sleepy, and a lullaby may not be what you need.

On the other hand, if you're overexcited before a certain hot date, that lullaby may be just what you need to calm you down, so you can focus and keep those feet on the ground.

21

• Finding Your • Inner Monologue

An actor's Inner Monologue consists of the thoughts that the actor's character is thinking to himself when he's not speaking aloud. This silent script can either be improvised once the actor is on stage, or written out by him before he gets there. The Russian acting teacher, Sonia Moore, had me write down the exact thoughts I was going to have on stage when I wasn't saying my lines. It seemed hard work, but very often it really paid off, keeping me both in character and in the moment.

Sometimes, if a scene is easy for an actor, he'll just listen. But sometimes, to make sure he stays on track, he will have decided exactly what he will be thinking at any given moment, even the images he will be seeing, and he will have written it all down.

Sometimes an actor's own thoughts or "inner monologue" will usurp his character's Inner Monologue, and he might be thinking "I hate this other actor, he's upstaging me," or "I hate her, I think she's sleeping with my husband," or, "I hate this play, I wish I were home playing with my dog."

If the actor's dog really has nothing to do with the play, this thought could weaken his performance, make it less focused. It could get him out of character, or even make him lose his concentration.

IT WORKS FOR ACTORS, IT CAN WORK FOR YOU

Actors sometimes write out their Inner Monologue as part of their preparation for playing a role. That way they'll know what they're *supposed* to be thinking about, and not get lost thinking about what they're going to have for dinner.

Say you go to see *Hamlet* and Hamlet is throwing Ophelia on the ground, saying, "Get thee to a nunnery, go!"

Ophelia's Inner Monologue might be "I don't want to go to a nunnery, I want to marry you, you jerk." Or "This Hamlet is a sick puppy, what's happened to him?" Or "God my head hurts, where it hit the floor." And too bad if the actress is thinking, "This costume is too tight. I never should have had dessert for lunch." But we hope she is thinking *something,* and not just waiting, vacant eyed and stupid, for her cue to speak her next line.

Many people, for scenes in their lives, for job interviews, business meetings, family functions, find it helpful to know what their inner monologue might be, to keep *them* on track and present.

Your Inner Monologue, like an actor's, isn't necessarily written in stone, but it can at least give you a center from which to feel secure, from which you can improvise.

UNSPOKEN MANTRAS

A MANTRA IS basically a sound, or word, or series of words, which is meant to be repeated over and over. The ancient Hindus understood the benefits of such repetition. They believed, for example, that if you repeated the word "Om," which means peace, over and over, you would feel peaceful. Many people chant "Om" today and find that they do feel a sense of peace.

IT WORKS FOR ACTORS, IT CAN WORK FOR YOU

Many words and sounds have the power to change your sense of being and even your brain chemistry, whether they are spoken aloud or even silently to yourself as a silent affirmation.

Sound, we know, heals, as doctors prove daily using ultrasound machines on muscles and ligaments.

The power of the word has been documented at least as far back as the Bible. The Old Testament, written twenty-five hundred years ago, states, "God *spoke* and the world came into being." The Gospel of John, written five hundred years later, begins, "In the beginning was the *word*." All of which suggests that the word, with its magical union of breath, sound, and meaning, might even be responsible for life itself.

So it is not surprising that one of the most effective and occasionally most powerful of all the acting techniques is the repetition of a mantra, silently, in your head.

The trick, of course, is to find the *right* word, or phrase, or sentences, to keep you centered, or on track, or motivated. Like "Keeping dancing." Or "Have fun."

A GREAT FIRST ACT CURTAIN

SOMETIMES, AN ACTOR will have to perform a scene, and laugh or cry, and the laughter and tears come easily. The play speaks to him, informs him, and he's fine. When this doesn't happen, an actor will need to find an acting technique to help.

IT WORKS FOR ACTORS, IT CAN WORK FOR YOU

Sometimes, in life, as in art, it is helpful if you use an acting technique, especially if a scene doesn't come easily for you.

In my one-woman play, *Dear Nobody,* there's a highly charged and emotional scene that was hard for me. I'm playing the eighteenth-century English novelist Fanny Burney, and at the end of the first act, I have to be so sad that I make the audience cry (while Fanny is trying hard *not* to).

She has just been chosen to live at the court of King George III (the one who went mad and lost America in 1776). Her position is to be Second Keeper of the Robes to Queen Charlotte (known mainly for her ugliness).

Fanny does try to see the bright side. She would, for example, get to share a carriage with the First Keeper of the Robes. But she will also have to leave her home, her friends, and the writing that makes her feel real, alive, and herself. Not that she would have put it like that. In fact, the eighteenth century words she speaks are so convoluted and dense, and her despair and fear so great, that without some special technique, there was no way I could have played the scene convincingly.

I finally decided that for Fanny's painful good-bye to the life she had loved, I would have to use a time in my own life when I had had to say good-bye to a man I had wanted to marry. So I not only used Sense Memory and saw this man's face in front of me during the scene, but I also gave myself the Inner Mantra, "Say good-bye. Say good-bye," and I kept repeating it to myself, until I truly felt, along with Fanny and the audience, the terrible pain of that good-bye.

Of course *you* don't need to leave your audiences crying, or want to be crying yourself. But I think this is a perfect example of an actor using an Inner Mantra that always got me the results I needed, centered me, focused me, and galvanized my energy.

Not bad for simply repeating two words in my head.

And you can use an Inner Mantra in your life so that can you actually feel good.

SALLY KEEPS IT TOGETHER

WHEN SALLY, A thirty-seven-year-old management consultant, came to me, what seemed to be bothering her most were the fights she had with her boyfriend. Usually, if she felt he was criticizing her, she would get defensive, he would raise his voice, and then she would start to fall apart, feel like she was disappearing, and want to cave in. Instead, she'd end up screaming back at him, or bursting into tears. She knew these histrionics could potentially sabotage her relationship. They had sabotaged her relationships before.

Not surprisingly, when she was a child, there had been a lot of screaming in her home. This had made her feel as if her world could crumble, as if there were nothing in her life to depend on, and even as if her life were in danger. The wonderful truth, though, was that now, with her boyfriend, she had a man she could depend on. Granted, he was yelling, but now her life was *not* in danger.

Unfortunately, her *relationship* was in danger, and she was afraid that she would either throw in the towel, or have so many tantrums that her boyfriend would split. And another relationship would be over.

It was an Inner Mantra that helped Sally not only to survive the fights, but even, occasionally, to avoid them. Because now, when she finds herself about to fall into a screaming match with her boyfriend, instead of automatically feeling helpless and yelling at him, she consciously buttons up her little lips and hears one, or any combination, of the following: "I really love this person. I am going to hear his point of view." "I am going to keep my mouth shut and listen to what he has to say." "Remember, Sally, he really loves you."

Especially hearing "He really loves you" seems to bring her into the present, and help her bypass her usual MO of screaming, crying, and generally sabotaging the relationship. It certainly makes her look a lot more attractive—if not to her boyfriend, at least to herself.

Would this, or some variation of Sally's sentences, allow *you* to feel and act more gracefully in a fight or confrontation? What Inner Mantras might work for *you*?

USING INNER MANTRAS TO GET A JOB OR A RAISE

NATURALLY, A JOB interview can be stressful. Mantras can help you get that job or get that raise. Of course you'll be a little nervous, but there's no reason that your fear should paralyze you or in any way sabotage your meeting.

Remember, when fear and excitement are photographed, they look like the same energy. Your fear simply anticipates a negative outcome from the interview, based on some incident from your past that ended badly, whereas your excitement anticipates a wonderful outcome, because of some incident from your past that ended well.

**IT WORKS FOR ACTORS,
IT CAN WORK FOR YOU**

Hearing an Inner Mantra in your head before and even during an interview can allow your unconscious to let go of old negative tapes and images, so you can be positive and excited and get that job or raise.

Here are some Inner Mantras, also known in the world of psychology as "affirmations" or "positive self-talk." They have worked for many of my clients. Play around with them. Maybe one, or even some of them, will work for *you*.

- ❑ "I'm excited to be here."
- ❑ "I deserve this job." Or "I deserve this raise."

❏ "I'm allowed to be calm and self-assured."
❏ "It's safe to be calm and self-assured."
❏ "It's safe to enjoy my life."
❏ "It's safe to have fun."
❏ "My interviewer is not my punishing parent."
❏ "I'm allowed to make more money than my father or mother."
❏ "I'm here to get the job, not to get love."
❏ "I will not die if I do not get this job or raise."
❏ "It's safe for me to be successful."
❏ "I know success is fun."
❏ "F—— you, I'm here to have fun."
❏ "I'm excited and it's safe."
❏ "I'm even sexually excited and it's safe." (Excited is excited.)

ROBERT'S PARTY MANTRA

Robert, a forty-year-old psychotherapist, felt it was important that he go to parties and meet new people, but when he did go, he tended to freeze up. This was not fun for him. In fact, occasionally, it was agony.

It turned out that Robert had a lot of friends, but when he went to a party, if his friends weren't there, he suddenly felt invisible and undesirable. He felt as if everyone at the party were better than he was, as if no one would want to talk to him, as if he didn't, in fact, have a lot of friends who cared about him and thought that he was wonderful. Which he was. But at those parties he just forgot.

I asked Robert to tell me about his best friends. I wrote their names down: Alice, Mark, Amy, David, Ellen, and Allen. He didn't list them in that order, but we eventually put them in that order so we could make him an acronym for a mantra.

We used the first letter of the first name of six of his friends, and came up with the word "Amadea," (*A*lice, *M*ary, *A*my, *D*avid, *E*llen, *A*llen).

I asked him to start repeating it, and asked him how it felt.

He said it a few times, eventually, almost like an incantation. Somehow it inspired him. And it made him smile, which is not surprising, since every time he mouthed a sound, he was remembering some friend who was very precious to him, who, he knew, loved him very much. No wonder it felt good.

As he repeated the word over and over, the mantra evolved into a kind of melody, which he ultimately had great pleasure singing. I suggested he sing it to himself in his car, on the way to his next party. I suggested he sing it, silently, to himself, once he got to the party, so he could remember who his friends were, to remind himself that he did indeed *have* friends. So that his friends could be, in a sense, with him. I suggested he chant that mantra to himself as often as he could, so he wouldn't feel as though he'd been abandoned or rejected (guess what had happened to him when he was small), or that he was unloved or unwanted, and so he wouldn't perpetuate the myth that he was.

So he had been rejected. The trick here was to find him a fast way to remember that this was no longer his reality, and to plug him into what his life was about *now*. The mantra did the trick.

See if it's a technique that works for *you*.

22

• Making the Most • of Your Voice

Many people come to me thinking that their voices don't have enough color, range, or resonance. They're right.

Maybe you have wanted to know how to give *your* voice more color, range, and resonance. The answer is "Practice." The same way you get to Carnegie Hall.

But you can make it fun. Play with your voice: maybe think of it as a new toy. Play games with it, and have a good time.

If you notice that you tend to use the same booming voice all the time, with no variation, consciously try using gentler colors. Try talking as if you were talking to a little wounded bird. Say to it, "I'm sorry you're hurt. But I know you'll be all right." Or imagine that you're talking to a wounded child.

VOCAL VARIETY

Any actor reciting Hamlet's soliloquies has to know how to put variety into those speeches, or his audience will fall asleep, or worse, throw tomatoes. Nobody wants tomatoes. Nobody wants to put his audience to sleep.

Lawyers are not the only people who need both to hold an audience captive and win, too. We all need to win.

So, how do you put unexpected, vivid colors into your vocal delivery?

Experiment.

What voice would you use if you were talking to a rapist? To your favorite movie star? To a dead man? To someone you wished were dead? To someone you wanted to seduce? To someone you *didn't* want to seduce?

Pick up a newspaper and start reading it out loud. Read anything, articles, even advertisements, anything. Give yourself a list of colors to use while you're reading and use a different color every two paragraphs. Your list of colors might include:

- ❑ Booming, confidant
- ❑ Timid
- ❑ Silly
- ❑ Unctuous, supplicating
- ❑ Charming, funny
- ❑ Musical, lilting
- ❑ Belching, farting
- ❑ Flirtatious
- ❑ Cloying
- ❑ Scared
- ❑ Tired

You may not ever consciously choose to use your list— particularly if you're a lawyer presenting a case. But you might as well play around with as many possibilities as you can, so that you can both get a good workout and begin to discover the limits of your instrument. Which might well be very nearly limitless.

Once you begin to have some control over your different voices, you can begin to choose when you want to use them. You'll use your more resonant voices for business presentations, your sexier ones for bed. Unless you want your business meeting to end in bed. In which case, you should probably think again.

For more variety, you could start imitating other people's voices:

- ❑ Your friends' voices (not necessarily to their faces)
- ❑ Your favorite teachers'
- ❑ A favorite actor's
- ❑ The voice of any President of the United States
- ❑ Daffy Duck

Open up your voice. Play with it. Own it. Really start to enjoy it.

And while you're playing around with different voices, try to feel where in your body they resonate, so that eventually you achieve maximum resonance. How many parts of your body can *you* feel resonating?

- ❑ Can you feel your chest cavity vibrating with sound?
- ❑ What about your head? Try to feel a high, loud "Eeee" vibrating about an inch above your eyebrows in the middle of your head.
- ❑ Make a loud "Haaah" sound and try to feel it resonate in your stomach.
- ❑ Try to feel it in your pelvis. Move with it. This could be exciting.

ROAR LIKE A LION

TRY ROARING LIKE a Lion. Make a big sound.

Open your mouth wide and roar. It's actually easy to do. Act As If you're a lion. Feels good, doesn't it, feeling that power?

John, a twenty-seven-year-old sign maker, came to one of my

workshops. He was shy and unhappy at how small his voice was. I suggested he try Roaring Like a Lion.

At first, he sounded like a very timid lion. But as I and the other people in the group encouraged him, his lion's voice got louder and louder, and, to his surprise and delight, no one wanted to punish him for making so much noise. He even began to enjoy himself.

More important, his voice began to change and he began to like his voice. John's voice had been very soft and slightly scratchy until he started Roaring Like a Lion. Somehow Roaring Like a Lion had freed him and his voice. Who knows why. Maybe he was a lion in another life. If he'd been a buffalo, we might have had to keep searching.

Anyway, when John thought Lion, he went crazy. Sounds came out of him that he never knew he had, that he never dreamed he had. And he started to feel terrific.

Then he started bringing his lion to business meetings. A little roar in the middle of any presentation does tend to get people' s attention, not to mention, wake everybody up. So what if they thought he was odd. Just as long as John made great signs, delivered them on time and cut a great deal, why should anybody have cared if he seemed a little odd. Unless, of course, they happened to be a little jealous.

I naturally suggest you roar with discretion and taste. John roared, and not only did his voice improve, but he began to think of himself as both bigger and more powerful than before he had started roaring. Let's face it, lions are bigger and more powerful than most average humans. John was beginning to allow himself to be all he could be, first vocally, then in other ways. With more voice came more self-assurance, more height, more presence, more self-respect. More John.

See what Roaring Like a Lion can do for you. And if the lion doesn't work, you can always try a buffalo.

MORE TRICKS TO ENRICH YOUR VOICE

A FEW YEARS ago, I had an audition for a musical, for which I was going to sing "Can't Help Loving That Man of Mine," which I knew the auditioners wanted to hear sung in a rich, full, big voice.

When I vocalized, I did have a rich, full, big voice. But the sounds that were coming out of my mouth as I tried to rehearse the song were thin, pinched, and neither as attractive nor as big as I knew I could make.

I'd been taking singing lessons for years, and knew technically what to do to make a big beautiful sound. Breathe from my stomach. Balance word with breath. Spit my consonants. Relax my body. You name it. But I tensed when I got to the words. Somehow, having to spend so much time with each word, because the words were sung instead of spoken, made me freeze as an actress.

I went to my acting teacher at the time, the brilliant Sandra Seacat. She somehow intuited to tell me simply to imagine I was at the ocean. Sensorily, of course. I worked at *seeing* the ocean, *smelling* the ocean, until I was breathing with the ocean, and I practically *was* the ocean.

I could hardly believe the sounds that came out of my mouth. They were rich, full, and very loud. It hardly sounded like my voice. But it was.

IT WORKS FOR ACTORS, IT CAN WORK FOR YOU

If you find the right acting technique, you can change your whole body's way of working, talking, singing, and sounding.

Imagining I was Maria Callas might have worked. Imagining I was talking to my niece might have worked. They've worked for me in other instances. But for that Gershwin tune, imagining I was at the ocean was what worked, and was a lot more effective than mentally reminding myself of a lot of vocal techniques that my body obviously couldn't manage all at once.

One of my students only has to think of herself as an egret, and she stands up straight and her stomach pulls in, and her posture is everything anyone could want it to be. Imagining she's an egret works much more effectively for her than telling herself, "Pull in your stomach," or "Pull back your shoulders," or "Don't slouch."

Is there some image that might help you to get *your* voice the way you want it? Remember, the body often responds better to images than to verbal commands.

What if you imagined yourself at the helm of a boat, calling to the sunset? Does your voice sound different? Richer? Fuller?

Play around with images and listen to what you can come up with.

PETER PLAYS CLARENCE DARROW

PETER, A TWENTY-NINE-YEAR-OLD lawyer, came to me because he knew he could present himself in court more effectively than he was doing.

Peter was an intelligent, sensitive man, who clearly had a good grasp of the cases he was presenting, but the impression he gave was not one of strength or conviction. His voice, in particular, sounded weak and thin.

I had Peter do the vocal warm-ups from Part One, and then some sensory exercises. Then I suggested he try playing a famous lawyer.

He chose Clarence Darrow.

Peter's transformation was immediate. Who knows what he had read or imagined about the famous lawyer. Who knows if he had even been him in another life. Who cares.

By simply telling himself he *was* Clarence Darrow, Peter's whole body changed. His chest was no longer sunken, his shoulders fell back, and best, his voice suddenly took on deeper, stentorian tones that neither of us had even guessed he had in him.

Not bad for simply Playing a Character.

IT WORKS FOR ACTORS, IT CAN WORK FOR YOU

Is there some character *you* could play that would automatically change *your* voice? Susan B. Anthony? Franklin Delano Roosevelt? Gomer Pyle?

23

• Speaking the Truth •

THERE ARE TIMES when Speaking the Truth can be a very powerful weapon. It is no accident that for centuries people have said, "Speak the truth and shame the devil." (And maybe the devil is only the fear or negativity or inhibition in your life.)

We're trained to be polite, which often means to lie. We do this so people will like us. So people will hire us. So for starters, we're not trained to Speak the Truth.

The first step in learning to Speak the Truth is to learn to tell the whole truth and nothing but the truth to yourself. About yourself. About your life. About how you feel. Without shame.

As children, many of us are encouraged not to say how we feel, not to cry, not to be afraid, or to admit to anybody that we're afraid. Including to ourselves. For many parents who can't deal with their own feelings, their children's feelings are simply overwhelming.

In Part One, in the chapter on your Emotional Preparation, I describe ways to discover how you feel. After you know the truth of how you feel, the trick is only to say it to the right person at the right time and place.

Knowing when not to speak the truth is also a valuable asset. Saying "I think you're ugly" is not, I believe, a useful thing to say. Particularly to your boss. Looking at someone's artwork and saying "I feel like throwing up" doesn't, in my opinion, help anyone either. (On the other hand, people can only love you if you say it in a moving vehicle before throwing up all over them.)

Practice saying how you feel. Practice saying it to yourself, to your reflection in a mirror, or to another person, "and the truth shall set you free."

TOM HANKS AND ROD STEIGER

PEOPLE TEND TO be moved by hearing the truth, and even to remember exactly when they heard it, whether it's someone saying "I love you" to them for the first time, or someone speaking the truth in a movie or a play. For one thing, it doesn't happen all that often.

Here is a story I love about Tom Hanks, winner of the Academy Award for his brilliant performances in *Philadelphia* and *Forrest Gump*. He was asked what comedy and drama have in common and he answered, "Ultimately it all comes down to telling the truth."

Then there's Rod Steiger's performance in *The Pawnbroker*, for which he more than deserved his Academy Award nomination. I know of many people who will never forget Rod Steiger's face and sobbing as he lies on the sidewalk at the climax of the movie. He's lost his shop, and his future, and he simply despairs. His face seems a reflection of all the pain and loss anyone could experience as a human being.

Steiger was, in fact, imagining the possible death of his own child, and was not only feeling, but also expressing what would be, for him, the truth of such a horror. It even feels as though he is expressing the universal truth of such a horror. And in that moment, he achieves a naked vulnerability and total honesty that most actors only dream of realizing—which is why so many people I know will never forget it.

ANDREA MARCOVICCI SINGS

I REMEMBER THE first time I saw Andrea Marcovicci perform. This wonderful actress and singer was up on a big stage and suddenly she said in this little girl voice: "Am I doing okay? I hope I'm doing okay."

She admitted she was afraid, and was so charming Speaking the Truth, so authentic and real, that her audiences were totally won over.

More important, she knew that once she had said she was afraid, her fear would dissipate. And it did. Then she could sing her songs freely, openly, expressively, and with all the power of who she is as a singer, actress, and person. Because she could be truthful about who she was at that moment and not hide.

See if admitting you're afraid doesn't break the ice for *you,* or at least allow you to feel more comfortable than you did before you said how you felt.

TELLING YOUR FRIENDS THE TRUTH

IT ALWAYS AMAZES me how uncomfortable people get simply by not daring to Speak the Truth. In any relationship. Business. Friendship. Whatever.

If we're carrying unspoken sentences around inside of us, and working our heads and bodies off trying to pretend we're not feeling something we're actually feeling, that's exhausting, and it's going to take energy, concentration, and truth away from whatever situation we're in.

Jenni, a thirty-year-old real estate broker, had a friend named Kimberly. One day, Kimberly had said, probably in jest, and certainly affectionately, that she thought Jenni was "crazy."

Unfortunately "crazy" was a button for Jenni. When Jenni was a child, her parents, it turned out, had called her "crazy" when they were angry at her: Jenni had always been afraid that it meant they'd send her to an institution. It took a certain amount of courage for her to tell Kimberly the truth, that it had upset her when Kimberly had called her "crazy."

When Kimberly realized how much she had upset Jenni, she apologized and said she had meant nothing by it, that for her, it had been simply a joke, even a term of endearment, and, most important, she would be careful not to do it again.

Although telling Kimberly the truth had been difficult and embarrassing for Jenni, she was surprised, relieved, and happy with Kimberly's reaction. When Jenni had told people how she felt when she was growing up, she had often been punished. But now it felt so good, she decided to try it again.

Kimberly seemed to love to give Jenni advice. Actually, Kimberly thought Jenni wanted it, or that, as a friend, she was supposed to "fix" her friends' problems or no one would like her. The truth was that Jenni didn't enjoy her advice at all.

One day Jenni finally told Kimberly the truth. "I wish you wouldn't give me advice," she said. "I just need to air what I'm feeling. It's my way of finding out what to do."

"Oh. Okay," Kimberly said, "I'll try not to do it again. I didn't know it upset you. I'm sorry. It's what my mother always does to me. And it drives me crazy."

The quality of Jenni's life improved radically as she learned to tell her friend the truth. Each time, she was sure she would say something that would make Kimberly never want to speak to her again. But each time she spoke the truth, Jenni found that she and Kimberly only got closer, the friendship grew richer and deeper, and Jenni was having more fun and was more comfortable being not only with Kimberly but also with herself.

Where could Speaking the Truth make *your* life better?

- ❑ At your job?
- ❑ At a party?
- ❑ With your boss?
- ❑ With your lover?
- ❑ With a friend?

24

• The Inner Walnut •

THE INNER WALNUT is an amazingly powerful tool, and it's my favorite technique in this book. I've been teaching it to people for twenty years and sometimes this is the only technique they need in order to look and feel powerful at a presentation, or to look and feel however they want wherever they happen to be.

The wonderful acting teacher Walter Lott taught me the technique when he coached me for a performance of my one-woman play, *Dear Nobody.* I was going to perform it in UCLA's Royce Hall. Not only does the theater have over a thousand seats, but it was the first time L.A. would see my work, and I felt I was auditioning for every movie mogul in Hollywood. It turned out I wasn't, but I was nervous.

In *Dear Nobody* I play both the eighteenth-century English novelist Fanny Burney, and thirty-six of her friends and acquaintances.

Walter asked me: "Why do you think you can play this part better than anyone else? What quality is it in you that makes you feel that?"

I thought for a while and then said "My love of Fanny and of the other characters. It's my ability to love. It's also the way she loves all the characters she describes."

"Good," he said. "Now find a symbol of that love."

I saw a heart, I think it was velvet. I thought this was a bit simplistic and obvious, but Walter said it was fine. He told me to go out on that stage and see that symbol, that heart, on and off during the performance. He said I could put it either inside or outside of me.

I did what he suggested, and that performance was possibly the best I have ever done of that play. People who saw it still talk about. It was a powerful experience for all of us. The performance took on a new breadth, intensity, strength, and fullness that it had never had before. I had never felt an audience so hushed. It was as if we had all been transported to another realm.

Why do I call this technique the Inner Walnut? Because when I used it again, I somehow found myself putting the symbols I came up with into a walnut shell and then the walnut into my heart. Why a walnut? I don't know. Maybe because the walnut is shaped like a heart. I was probably looking for something to contain the symbol. What matters is that the technique always helps me, and has helped countless others.

So how do you use this technique in your life?

Sometimes, when I want to be funny and make people laugh, I ask for a symbol of my sense of humor. Sometimes I'll get Bugs Bunny. Then I'll put that little rascal into a walnut shell and into my heart, and I am suddenly, magically buoyed. I start being funny and start having a good time. Why? Because a symbol is a powerful thing.

THE POWER OF SYMBOLS

WHAT I'M ASKING you to do is to find a symbol and in a sense meditate on it. I've discussed the power of meditation to change your body chemistry. We're only adding a symbol.

Symbols have been used for thousands of years to focus and strengthen the people who use them. Religions have always used them, like the cross in Christianity and the Star of David in Judaism.

IT WORKS FOR ACTORS, IT CAN WORK FOR YOU

Meditation on a symbol, with or without any sensory component, has always been a powerful tool for self-transformation.

In his writing, the famous psychoanalyst Carl Jung has documented the symbols used by cultures all over the world as tools for healing and wholeness. He explains and describes how symbols feed us and fortify our spirit, how their shape and meaning resonate with something deep inside us. Symbols possess archetypal energy, so that if you choose to meditate on, for example, a crystal as a symbol for mental clarity, you will be able to access Crystal Clarity everywhere.

So here's the exercise:

- ❑ Sit, palms up on your thighs, or lie down, arms at your sides.
- ❑ Take three deep breaths.
- ❑ Think of some talent, quality, or strength that you have, that you know to be uniquely yours. Perhaps it's your ability to think clearly, or to be kind, or to persevere.
- ❑ Ask for an image to come to you that symbolizes this strength or talent. Usually the first image that comes to you is perfect. The idea is not to analyze here. We're in right-brain, nonlogical terrain.
- ❑ Put the symbol into a walnut shell and put it in your heart.
- ❑ Feel that symbol vibrating inside your chest for difficult situations.

- ❑ Or see the symbol anywhere at all—in the air next to you or on the wall opposite you.
- ❑ Whatever you're doing, wherever you are, from time to time, remember it is there.

This technique can give you a special inner grounding and focus as well as inspire you. By putting that walnut in your heart, and feeling the symbol vibrating there, you're forced to feel your body, which most of us will either ignore or leave behind when we're nervous, and there goes the subconscious knowledge that our body is there to defend us should we need it.

For a wonderful example of someone using the Inner Walnut, see the section on Public Speaking in chapter 25, where it is used by a priest.

· Real-Life · Challenges

PART FOUR

So now *you're ready to go out into the real world!*

You've learned twenty-four different acting techniques to use in difficult situations and this is your chance to play around with them. And I hope you will "play" around with them and not stress over them, or beat yourself up if you don't think you're using them perfectly. These techniques take time and practice, but they do work, as you'll see in the stories that follow in Part Four.

You'll read more stories about non-actors who have used the techniques both to improve how they function in their lives and to improve the quality of their lives—from a businesswoman who wanted to be more feminine and sensual with her husband to an Episcopalian priest anxious to give more inspiring sermons. These stories show how acting techniques can help you through many of your real-life challenges.

The real challenge though, it seems to me, is to enjoy our lives as much as possible, no matter what cards we've been dealt. This, as I hope you've now experienced, is what these techniques are really all about.

25

• Public Speaking •

According to numerous surveys, public speaking inspires more terror in the hearts of men than death itself, so I'm devoting a whole chapter to it, including a section on stage fright, which is what actors call the terror that anyone can experience who has to appear or speak in public.

STAGE FRIGHT: ON STAGE AND IN LIFE

Most actors experience stage fright at some point in their careers before they go on stage. Even the great Sir Laurence Olivier suffered it—not always, but suddenly and for a short and painful period of time, quite a while after he had been acknowledged as possibly the greatest actor of his time. And then he could just barely get himself to go out onto the stage. He'd throw up. People would literally have to push him on stage.

In time, he got over it. And so can you.

Olivier's body was acting, or rather reacting, as if there might have been hungry lions out in the audience. Logically, of course, we all know there are probably no lions out there. But when we get afraid, our bodies react as if there were. That's what stage fright is: the body acting as if its life were in danger, and our adrenaline starts flowing and our muscles tighten and our throats dry up. But there is no danger.

This irrational fear of an audience full of strangers is based on long repressed fears from childhood, maybe from when some grown-up got angry if we didn't perform perfectly, when we knew our survival depended on their feeding us, and we feared they might withhold our food, and we would die.

Our bodies' system of inter-linking nerves and memories works in such a way that sometimes, when even a tiny little fear has been awakened in us, all our old fear memories and feelings will kick in and produce a kind of domino effect.

We experience this more obviously when we lose someone we love, and simultaneously, unwillingly and unconsciously (often the same thing), we experience all the losses of love that we have suffered in our lifetime.

That's how we are wired and the way memories are stored in the body—which is why, in his amazing series of novels the *Remembrance of Things Past,* Marcel Proust was able to recreate twenty years of experience simply from the smell of a sugar cookie that he used to eat as a child. Our old fears are ignited and magnified in the same way.

If you suffer from any form of stage fright (or nerves), you probably have a few unconscious fear tapes that get triggered for no apparent reason. It's why we can be intimidated by some woman we don't even know, if she happens to be wearing the same perfume our old aunt Essie wore when she used to pinch our cheeks until they hurt, and we felt helpless to say, "Please don't pinch me like that. It hurts." We may not *consciously* recognize the perfume, but our body remembers, and automatically (or unconsciously), it tightens up.

Most of the acting techniques in this book give orders directly to the unconscious, which controls our involuntary physical behavior—like crying or sweating or shaking with fear, activities that actors are called on to do all the time, and which don't usually happen by our simply giving ourselves a mental order.

Rationally, we all know it's unlikely that our audience is going to devour us, or even throw tomatoes, or run us out of town. But that's what the fear *feels* like. That's what some unconscious fear tape, possibly of some childhood terror, is telling us. We have to give our unconscious a different tape to play, not the tape of some childhood terror, but a new tape to make us feel safe and loved.

LEARNING TO FEEL SAFE AND LOVED

HAVING STAGE FRIGHT is the opposite of feeling safe and loved.

Feeling safe and loved goes hand in hand with feeling good about yourself, feeling you're okay. Even knowing you're totally terrific. But feeling safe and loved seems to inspire the other feelings, and allows a performer to perform to the best of his ability. It's a feeling that makes a job interview easy or hard. Not to mention life itself.

Some actors, through the transformative magic of their gift, automatically feel safe and loved (both protected and able to protect themselves) simply because they are on a stage or in front of a camera. Sometimes it's the only place they *do* feel safe and loved, because many actors suffer from stage fright in life. Ironically, sadly, many actors feel safe and loved only when they're acting. This used to be true, to a great extent, for me. Garbo's shyness was, of course, legendary. The great Brando, too, is known to be shy.

Ideally, we'd all feel safe and loved all the time. Using the acting techniques in this book can help. When I remember to use them, *I* feel safe and loved.

Of course, if you're giving a speech, knowing what you're supposed to say can help you begin to feel safe. And you can feel loved by using, well, everything from the neck massage in your

Physical Preparation, to a Sense Memory of someone loving you, or your best friend's singing "Happy Birthday" to you.

What makes *you* feel safe and loved? Is it imagining you're at that brook in the country, with the sun shining on you, and the birds singing? If so, then bring it to the hall where you'll be giving that speech. If it's imagining your lover kissing you on the eyes, then bring those lips onto the podium with you. Is it your watchdog? Then put him, or two, or three of him, out in the audience. Remember, your body won't know the difference between your real dog and an imaginary one.

A PRIEST TALKS TO HER PARISH

HELEN, A FORTY-EIGHT-YEAR-OLD Episcopal priest, could be a secure and even riveting speaker when she knew or felt that her audience was with her and understood her.

But Helen was a mystic by nature, and she knew that some of the spiritual concepts that she wanted to share with her audiences were occasionally too liberal for some of her listeners, and therefore, not always well received or even understood. Knowing this often made her nervous and uncomfortable when she most wanted to be strong and inspiring.

She came to me because she felt she was letting herself and others down by occasionally not speaking of the mysticism about which she was passionate.

Helen knew she was letting both the real, and worse, her *imaginary* judges out in the audience silence her, as if she were a little girl and their disapproval threatened her life. She needed a technique to help her believe that her audience was, instead, full of people who would listen openly and receptively, even approvingly and lovingly.

We needed to find her a technique that would relax her and make her feel safe and loved, so she could preach what she truly believed, in an inspired way.

I asked Helen if she had some best friend she could imagine, with Sense Memory, out in the audience. It turned out there was a friend of hers, a priest, who she felt understood her and with whom she easily shared her ideas. I suggested she imagine he was in the back of the audience, and that she talk to him.

Helen tried this and began to loosen up. But to really feel safe, she needed to put her friend all over the room, in the front row, in the back, by the windows, and on the podium, and I knew we could come up with something better.

In the end, it was the technique called the Inner Walnut that worked best for her (see Chapter 24 on the Inner Walnut).

When Helen closed her eyes and thought of the one talent, quality, or strength that she felt was unique about herself, she chose her ability to find oneness with God. When she asked for a symbol of this oneness, an image of St. Michael appeared to her. For Helen, St. Michael represented not only man's ability to end war on earth, but also his ability to transform our earthly war zone into God's perfect heaven. For her, St. Michael symbolized man's ability to become one with the world, the heavens and God, just as it was Helen's core desire and talent to feel that oneness and to communicate it as a priest.

After Helen saw the image of St. Michael, she imagined it fitting into a walnut shell, and put it into her heart. I asked her to feel the energy, pulse, and power of the image vibrating at her center, and to speak only after she felt it. When she spoke, her voice had a new depth and resonance. She was expressing a strength and centeredness that she had never expressed before. We were both thrilled.

Now Helen has a far more conscious, effective, comforting and even inspiring focus for her attention than those first real or imaginary judges that she had felt were out in the audience. And when she stands before a congregation with members who may be less mystical than herself, she doesn't feel intimidated anymore or blocked. She can communicate from her heart what she truly feels. She feels good about this and probably more of her listeners are going to understand what she is saying than if she were not so focused, inspired, and secure from feeling the symbol of St. Michael at her heart.

GIVING A PASSIONATE PRESENTATION

HOW DOES AN actor perform with great passion, if he's talking about something that doesn't even interest him all that much? (Or, as Hamlet says about one of the actors who comes to the Danish court, "What's Hecuba to him or he to Hecuba that he should weep for her?")

How does an actor bring truth and passion to a character who is obsessed with cows or spinach or San Salvador, if cows or spinach or San Salvador mean nothing to him?

IT WORKS FOR ACTORS, IT CAN WORK FOR YOU

How do you bring *your* passion to a business presentation or a legal defense, if you're out of sorts, or worried about something else, or worse, you just don't *feel* any passion for your subject? Substitution and Imagination.

Say you're giving a speech in order to raise money and you've given it 998 times, and you're tired of it, how do you get fired up for the 999th time?

Worse, what if you have to get passionate about a financial proposal and numbers bore you, not to mention you'd rather be out fishing. Or what if you're a lawyer and need to sound as if you believed, passionately, in whatever your arguments were, if you, too, would rather be out fishing. And you can't afford to be out fishing.

The answer is to find your *own* passion, and substitute that for the subject about which you're lukewarm.

Let's say you've just read about a six-year-old girl who's been terribly abused, and you're horrified and outraged and you believe, passionately, that there should be more laws to prevent such abuse.

When you give your presentation the trick might be to see an image of that girl on the wall across from you when you need to get in touch with your passion. You might think about her when you take a deep breath, so that your passion for reform would flow into your presentation.

Of course, it's best to find a topic that relates, at least tangentially, to your presentation. But if, for example, the little girl were six years old, and the financial proposal you are giving has a lot of sixes in it, then, every time you come to one of them, you could think of that child, feel your righteous fury, and go back to those numbers with renewed vigor, commitment, and passion.

KIM READS HER STORY OUT LOUD

KIM, A TWENTY-TWO-YEAR-OLD Japanese American young woman, had just graduated from college. She had taken one of my workshops and called me one day for help.

Kim had always dreamed of becoming a professional writer and had been writing short stories for a long time. She had finally gotten one accepted for publication, and it had even won an award. She called me because she had accepted an invitation to read it out loud in front of forty people and she was scared.

Not only was Kim not used to speaking in public, not only was her cultural heritage one of quiet good manners, but she was faced with what for her was an even more difficult task: to expose herself publicly as an artist and a writer.

I asked her what her story was about.

"Two young children in Hiroshima after the bombing," she answered.

I asked what she thought the meaning of her story was.

She said it was the horrific effect of the bomb on young life.

"If there were a symbol," I said, "of what you wanted to say in that story, a symbol of your passion when you wrote it, of what you wanted to communicate with your audience, what would it be?"

She thought for a while and then said, "It's a river."

I could tell from the emotion in her voice that she had found the right symbol.

She began to speak quickly—about how the river that flowed through Hiroshima symbolized for her, both in the story and in her imagination, the need of the victims to speak out; about how it was a symbol of the victims' outpouring, of the flow of their words and hers. She suddenly saw how it bridged the new town and the old, and saw it as a symbol of the children's connection to their past and present, and even as a symbol of the flow of life itself.

Kim said she was amazed that she hadn't really understood all this until she had had to answer my question. Even though she had written the story herself.

I told her that most playwrights I had known or read about were equally surprised by what their directors often helped them to see in the plays they had already written. As the writer, one is in the middle of the river of one's creation, but if, as in her case, the writer wants to perform the work, publicly, he or she has to step outside it and see it more objectively, as an actor would, in order to know what themes to emphasize, what colors to bring out, what passions to accent. I have written plays, and then acted in them. So I know.

A mind writing words is very different from a body performing them. Listen to most English and American poets reading their work out loud. Most end up reading in a monotone. The left side of the brain is word-oriented, intellectual, and rational, and totally opposite from the right side, which allows an actor to be physical, expressive, and full of passion.

For Kim, once we knew she was going to use the river, we needed to find out how. I suggested she try putting an image of some of the river into an Inner Walnut in her heart, or putting a sensory recreation of the river on the far wall of the room where she would be reading her story, so she could see it, hear it, smell it, taste it, and sense, with all her senses, its energy and flow, along with the flow of her own words and her passion to tell her tale.

There is, of course, great power in meditating on a symbol. Sometimes, a picture is worth a thousand words. Or can be. I knew that the river, an archetypal energy itself, would focus her, propel her, and support her. No matter how she used it.

A friend of hers had advised her to take some deep breaths before she started. To this suggestion, I added that she not only try breathing in the smell of the river, but also try breathing *with* the river, in time with its own music, flow, and breath.

"Think about the river *before* you have to read," I told her, "about what it means to you, and to the characters in your story. Think about how it symbolizes your passion. Because I have a feeling that once you start reading, your own strength, conviction, and belief in the importance of your story will carry you. And you'll be wonderful. You may only need to use the river as a Preparation. If you happen to tense up, or feel anxious, anytime during the reading, for whatever reason, because someone sneezes, or for no apparent reason at all, you can just go back to the river. To seeing it, feeling it, whatever."

And that's what Kim did.

And her reading not only went well, but she even enjoyed the experience.

BARRY PRIMUS SPEAKS IN PUBLIC

BARRY PRIMUS, A wonderful actor and director, knows how to translate the techniques he learned as an actor into skills he can use in his life.

He knows that the trick of public speaking (the same as the trick for overcoming self-consciousness) is to focus on anything but his insecurities, to focus on anything but how he imagines his audience is judging him.

So sometimes, if he has to give a talk, or even pitch a film, he says, "I'll think: how can what I'm doing bring something positive into the world, instead of doing it just for me? Then my nerves come down and I become focused. I feel I have a right to be there. If I can stop doing it for myself, and start doing it for the part of me which is making a contribution to the community, I become more courageous and it gets the attention off me, and the whole thing starts to become more spiritual and I can get behind it more, like a warrior or a soldier, because I realize it needs to be done."

IT WORKS FOR ACTORS, IT CAN WORK FOR YOU

Doing service for a greater good helps a lot of people to overcome their stage fright or self-consciousness for public appearances. It also helps them to feel good about themselves. Is it something that could help you, too?

26

• Overcoming Your • Self-Consciousness

PEOPLE COME TO me asking me what to do about their self-consciousness. They want to know how actors manage to forget about the hundreds or even millions of people that could be watching them at any given performance.

What is self-consciousness? Most often, a person who is self-conscious, as we usually understand the word, tends to be keenly and uncomfortably conscious of being watched and judged by others.

So, although their consciousness might seem to be on themselves, or on what they perceive to be "bad," "imperfect," or "awful" about themselves, their consciousness is, in fact, on what they imagine their judges are saying about them. In other words, "Is someone out there thinking that my hair is a mess?" Or "Is the audience throwing up at the sight of the pimple on my cheek?" Or "I wonder if anybody can tell that my dress is too tight." This kind of self-consciousness is basically *judge*-consciousness, and something nobody wants.

IT WORKS FOR ACTORS, IT CAN WORK FOR YOU

The antidote to judge-consciousness is being conscious of anything *but* the judges and what they might be saying.

Say Holly has just met Doug, and she fears that he is judging her hair, her nose, her makeup, whatever. The alternative to her focusing on his possibly negative judgments (her paranoid projections) is for her to become extremely conscious of—anything else. Maybe it's *his* nose, *his* hair, *his* suit. Maybe she likes them. Maybe she doesn't.

She could be conscious of anything, just as long as she chooses something specific for her focus. She could focus on a Magic Stone in her pocket, on a sensorily recreated waterfall on the wall opposite her, or on her favorite piece of music, which she could decide to hear in her head.

Actors know they would only be sabotaging their performances if they focused on the judgments their audiences might be making. So they, like our hypothetical Holly, consciously decide to concentrate on anything else. They could concentrate on a Sense Memory, on a Psycho-physical Action, or on a song in their head.

They could concentrate on other actors' faces, or on other actors' words. In other words, they could concentrate on Listening. Sir Anthony Hopkins has said he believes that listening is the most important thing an actor can do.

Most often, an actor will decide *before* he goes on stage what technique he'll use when he gets there. He won't always have to use it. If he's lucky and gets inspired, the scene will play itself, easily, fully, creatively, effortlessly. If only that could happen to all of us all the time. But it's nice to have something to fall back on—just in case.

HOW ACTORS OVERCOME THEIR SELF-CONSCIOUSNESS

YOU CAN USUALLY tell when an actor is worrying about how he or she looks. Their acting is postured and self-conscious. Worrying about how you look is another way of admitting that you are worried about what the judges will say about how you look.

I will have the grace here not to mention certain performances, which you may have seen, by actors who were more concerned about how they looked than about what they were saying or doing. (Although I can say that, at unfortunate moments in my own career, I have been one of them.)

Meryl Streep has said that for a close-up in a movie, she can be thinking of what she will make for lunch, and all the camera will register is that she is thinking. She is definitely not thinking of what the audience might be thinking about how she looks.

DAVID OBSERVES HIS BLIND DATE

DAVID, A FORTY-YEAR-OLD systems analyst, came to one of my workshops. He had spent most of his life feeling self-conscious. He said he felt particularly uncomfortable on the blind dates he would ask his friends to find him. The more potentially perfect the woman seemed, especially if she were beautiful, the harder it was for him to speak.

I had David do an Observation exercise, which seemed to help him a lot. This exercise is done with a partner, and went something like this.

First, I had him choose a partner and then I asked him to face her and exaggerate his old and painful self-consciousness by listing what his partner might be finding "wrong" with him. In other words, he projected his inner judge onto his partner and spoke his paranoid projections out loud.

"Does she see the spot on my shirt? Does she think I'm ugly?"

I stopped him. Enough is enough. David had been practicing this part of the exercise for most of his life.

What David *did* experience from focusing on his partner's imaginary judgments was the tension in his shoulders, the strangling of his neck, the muffled quality of his voice, and his general and total physical, psychological, and emotional discomfort.

I then asked him not to imagine how his partner might be criticizing him, but to concentrate instead on what he was conscious of in his partner. Only things he liked, of course.

He admired the color of her blouse, the whiteness of her teeth, the length of her eyelashes. He was so busy observing *her,* he didn't have time or space to imagine any judgments she might have been having about *him.*

For David's dreaded dates, I suggested he could also notice things that were not as complimentary as those he had noticed in the workshop, since the woman across the table from him would presumably not be hearing his list. Did he find her jewelry too garish, for example? Did she have a mustache?

I was not encouraging him to be mean, mind you, but only trying to make him conscious of where he was and what he was seeing and thinking, to take the focus off his imaginary judges, and to make him more real, alive, and in touch with himself and his reality. I was encouraging him to take back his eyes, instead of giving them away and quaking at being seen. I wanted him to be conscious of a self that was more real than the one he used to imagine was being mercilessly judged.

David started doing this exercise on his dates and he even started to have fun. For one thing, he was present, which always feels better and looks more attractive than vacant and terrified. Now when he goes out, he's at least no longer terribly uncomfortable and painfully self-conscious.

IT WORKS FOR ACTORS, IT CAN WORK FOR YOU

So, do *I* ever feel self-conscious? When I remember to use the techniques in this book, I'm always okay. Without them, I admit it—I can still sometimes flounder. Most people teach best what they most need to learn.

MARY'S SELF-CONSCIOUSNESS

Mary was a shy and quiet dental hygienist. She wasn't afraid to talk to children, but when she had to be with her older boyfriend's friends or associates, she became so self-conscious that she could barely talk. Mary was twenty-five, her boyfriend and his associates were all over fifty.

Intellectually, Mary knew that the likelihood of these people gunning her down was remote. But that was the level of her fear. She could even see this as a form of insanity. But she froze.

Mary explained to me that both she and her boyfriend were unhappy and uncomfortable that she wasn't able to hold her own at dinner parties, where she barely spoke a word. In fact, at our first session, Mary sometimes spoke so softly I had trouble hearing her at all.

Mary came to me for about ten sessions, and through a combination of techniques, she began to overcome the self-consciousness that made it so difficult for her to speak up.

At our first session, Mary and I talked, and it became clear that the way she froze at these dinners was not unlike the way she had frozen as a five-year-old at the dinner table with her mother and her stepfather. Apparently, her stepfather had repeatedly and loudly insisted that she "not interrupt" when he and her mother were talking. What Mary had felt he was saying was "Don't talk at all."

Her stepfather had been a threatening bully of a man. Mary had been intimidated by him, her mother had never spoken up for her, and now Mary seemed to be reliving the same dining-room scene every time she went out to dinner with her boyfriend and his friends. She simply regressed into playing herself at five, and everybody at the party became her stepfather, a man she knew would punish her for speaking, on whom she depended for her survival, and whom neither she nor her mother had ever dared to challenge.

MARY PLAYS HERSELF

I ASKED MARY to imagine herself as a little girl back at the dinner table with her mother and stepfather. Sensorily. I told her I wanted her to try and Play a Character: Herself at Five. I wanted her finally to say the words that she had never been allowed to speak then, the sentences that had gotten stuck in her throat, and stayed there for almost twenty years, that needed and were ready, finally, to come out.

Mary easily remembered what it was like to be five. She didn't have to imagine herself small or remember what she had been wearing. Some people have to, but Mary simply remembered how she had felt. After all, she had been there.

I asked the five-year-old Mary how she felt with her stepfather barking at her "not to interrupt."

Mary folded her arms in front of her and said, in a very quiet voice, "I don't like it."

I asked her to exaggerate the physical pose in an attempt to get her in touch with the feelings that she had had as a little girl.

Soon Mary had folded her arms as tightly around her as they would go.

"What do you think your little girl would have liked to say to your stepfather?" I asked.

Mary was quiet.

I made a suggestion. "What about 'I want to speak'?"

Mary nodded. As a child, of course, she had never dared to say a word. Now, slowly, quietly, she began.

"I want to speak," she said.

I urged her to keep going. "What else would you have liked to say to him? Maybe, 'I deserve to speak'?"

She nodded.

I asked her to repeat the phrases. "I want to speak. I deserve to speak."

Mary was speaking quietly. I stood up and moved away from her. "Try speaking louder," I said. "Change the words if you want, and speak louder."

"I deserve to speak. I have a right to speak." She was speaking a little louder now.

"Good," I said. "Again."

"I deserve to speak. I have a right to speak. I want to speak."

Every time Mary spoke the words, I moved a little farther from her, and asked her to speak a little louder. She was not comfortable speaking so loud. After all, as a child, she'd been threatened if she even spoke at all.

"You're doing well," I said. "What about, 'I'm going to speak and you can't stop me,' or, 'Don't interrupt me, I want to talk.'"

Mary liked the suggestions, and began to repeat the phrases.

"Don't interrupt me. I want to talk. I'm going to talk and you can't stop me."

"Good," I said, moving to the other end of the room. "Louder."

"I'm going to talk and you can't stop me!!!"

Little by little, her voice got louder and louder. She wasn't shouting yet, but she was beginning to enjoy a new freedom and the sound and strength of a voice she had been brought up never to speak or hear. Mary was finally ready to find her voice. After all those years.

I told her that her assignment for the week was to keep saying those sentences, or sentences like them, anytime she could, and as loudly as she could. In the car. In the kitchen. Anywhere.

When Mary came back the next week, her voice was just a little bit louder than it had been the week before. She had been speaking the sentences out loud in the shower. And she had been having a wonderful time.

MARY SPEAKS THE TRUTH

DURING THE WEEK after our third session, an old friend of Mary's, from her hometown in Ohio, came to visit her. One night, Mary, her boyfriend, and Mary's friend all went out to dinner, and Mary noticed that, every time she began to speak, her boyfriend interrupted.

Just as her stepfather had done so many years before.

Psychology has a name for recreating unresolved situations from our past, situations that we apparently recreate to make them finally come out right. It's called repetition compulsion. Whatever it's called, Mary saw the parallel between her being interrupted at the dinner table by her stepfather when she was five, and being interrupted by her boyfriend, twenty years later.

Mary had to Speak the Truth to her boyfriend, and tell him, as she had been unable to tell her stepfather, that it didn't help her if he interrupted.

Luckily, her boyfriend was open to hearing what Mary had to say. After all, it had been both his and her idea that she come see me in the first place. Unlike her stepfather, he listened to her. He apologized and said he would try not to interrupt her in the future.

This was another big step for Mary. But it had taken her many years to achieve her level of self-consciousness. It would not disappear overnight. Mary still needed a little more coaching.

MARY PLAYS HER GOOD MOTHER

AT ANOTHER SESSION, I again asked Mary to play herself at five at the dinner table with her mother and stepfather.

Again she heard her stepfather's roar; again she felt afraid.

Again I asked her to exaggerate, physically, how she was feeling, so that she could get in touch more deeply with how she had felt then.

She wrapped her arms tightly around herself, until she was almost coiled into a ball.

"How do you feel?" I asked.

"I'm scared," she said.

"Good," I said, "Tell me more."

"I'm scared to open my mouth. I'm scared my stepfather will hit me. I wish I were invisible. I don't want anybody to see me."

I asked her to talk about wanting to be invisible.

"I don't want anybody to see me. I wish I could hide."

The most exciting moments in the theater are when an actor follows his impulses. I asked Mary to follow her impulse to hide, to see if there weren't somewhere in the room where we were working where she could hide.

She pointed to a large desk that was against one of the walls. I nodded. Then she got up and crouched behind the desk. This was not easy for her, but she was doing well, and I told her so. I asked her to continue to stay with how she felt.

"I'm scared. I want to hide. I wish I were invisible." She was practically whimpering.

I suggested that these were possibly the feelings she had unconsciously been feeling when she had been so quiet at her boyfriend's dinners. Her body's logic had been perfect: you make no noise, so no one notices you, so no one hurts you.

Now it was time for Mary to play another role: Her Good Mother, the kind of mother that her own mother had never been able to be for her. Remember, when she was five, when Mary's stepfather had silenced her, Mary's real mother had never stood up for her or uttered a word.

I asked Mary to Act As If she were a really good mother, to play, in fact, the warmest, wisest, most loving, giving, and compassionate person she could imagine being. Mary understood these qualities, because she had needed them so desperately, growing up.

I asked her to stand up and play Her Good Mother. "Speak to that scared little girl on the floor," I said. "Tell her how you feel about how scared she is."

Mary stood up and looked behind the desk where she had been hiding as her five-year-old self. "I want you to talk, " she began.

"Good," I said. "Go on."

Mary was quiet.

"What else do you want to tell her?" I said softly.

"I'm sorry you're so scared," she said.

"Could you tell her you'll take care of her now, and won't let her be bullied anymore? Or that you know she's scared, but that now, she's safe?"

"I'll take care of you," Mary said.

"Good," I said. "Maybe tell her it's safe to talk now and you want her to talk, and you won't let anybody bully or hurt her ever again."

Mary continued, "No one's going to hurt you. It wasn't fair what they did to you, never letting you speak."

"Good," I said, encouraging her to go further. "How's your little girl look now?"

"Less scared."

"Is there anything else you want to tell her?"

Mary took a deep breath and said, "I love you. And I'm going to protect you." There were tears in her eyes.

I told Mary it was okay if she cried. I said I too thought it was sad that her little girl had never heard these words, or hadn't known it was safe to talk for all these years. I told her it was natural for her to feel sad, and to cry if she wanted. She did.

Then I said, "How's your little girl doing?"

She looked down to where she had been huddled on the floor. "Better," she said.

"How's she feeling?"

"She's happy."

"Does she want anything?" I asked.

"She wants a hug," Mary said.

I told Mary to imagine hugging her initially frightened little girl. Mary wrapped her arms around herself. She was smiling.

"How does it feel?" I asked.

"Good," she said. Her eyes were closed and she was beaming.

Later, for the dinner parties Mary had to go to with her boyfriend, I suggested she remember the words and voice of the good mother she had just played. Mary's problem at these parties had been that she had gotten stuck in the monologue of her terrified child, so it was useful for her to have, instead, words from Her Good Mother.

Soon, if Mary noticed herself getting tense or wanting to disappear, she talked, silently, as Her Good Mother, to her little five-year-old self, as she had done at our session.

Mary's self-consciousness continued to diminish.

MARY USES INNER MONOLOGUE

ONE NIGHT, AT one of Mary's boyfriend's dinners, everyone had been talking about politics in Africa and Mary had felt particularly awkward not being able to contribute. She began thinking, "How could I be so stupid? I know nothing about what they're talking about. They must really think I'm stupid because I'm not saying anything. I wish I could fall through a hole in the floor."

Mary had concentrated on how stupid she was feeling. I asked her if she couldn't have focused on something else.

It had never occurred to her to have thoughts based on her real feelings that, it turned out, went something like, "I really don't fit in. I wish they were talking about something I knew about or was more interested in. So what if I'm quiet. I know I'm intelligent. I can even be witty, strong, and loving. I'm good enough."

Or she could have figured out what her body was feeling and her Inner Monologue might have gone something like this: "My shoulders are tight. I need to breathe into my chest. My legs are crossed so that I'm constricting all the organs in the lower part of my body."

Obviously, any of these real thoughts would have made her life easier than it had been with her sitting there telling herself she was stupid.

Or Mary could have done a Sense Memory, felt her Magic Stone, or listened to Her Good Mother.

Or she could have just listened.

MARY'S PROGRESS AND THE ROSE

ONE DAY, MARY came to a session and said she had gone to a party but that it had been a disaster; she had been too quiet. Her boyfriend had said that he "understood," but they had both wished she had spoken more.

I asked her if she had, in fact, talked at the party at all.

Mary said she had.

I pointed out that when she had first come to me, she had had trouble saying anything at all at any party.

Mary admitted this was true.

I mentioned an epigram I often find helpful: "Progress, not perfection."

But Mary was upset and angry at herself because she hadn't been able to talk when her host had turned to her and said, "Well, Mary, tell us about Ohio."

She had felt on the spot, stupid, and even humiliated because she hadn't been able to come up with a story.

It was easy enough for us to prepare a story for Mary to tell at another time (if, in fact, she would feel that she had to tell any story at all if she was asked like that).

What concerned me more, however, was that she was being so hard on herself. I explained it was a little like planting a seed in the ground one day, and then yelling at it the next, because it wasn't yet a rose. A seed only becomes a rose if you water it. And then one day you'll see a little shoot pushing out of the ground. A little later, part of a stem. Then a bud.

I asked Mary if it didn't seem crazy to her if someone yelled at the little shoot, "Why aren't you a rose yet?" Or at the bud, the beautiful bud, "Why aren't you a full and open flower?"

I suggested that she not yell at herself for not having become the Conversationalist of the Year after only six sessions. And I suggested she focus on the fact that she had contributed at least *something* to the party. I reminded her of how self-conscious she had felt at parties when she had first come to me.

Working together over the next three months, Mary herself bloomed. She used the role-playing techniques I've described; she used Personalization, the Magic Stone, vocal exercises, and Substitution. Her self-confidence grew. She learned to speak up so that people could hear her and she even began to enjoy going out with her boyfriend. Little by little, her self-consciousness diminished.

What techniques in this book could help you deal with *your* self-consciousness?

27

• Social Gatherings •

DON'T BE HARD on yourself if you get nervous going to parties or business functions. We are, after all, social animals, and like animals, if we go into a strange place, our instinct is to be cautious, to sniff it out, to make sure it's a safe place for us to be.

Many people come to me who have no trouble being their charming, relaxed, casual selves in front of lovers, family, or friends, but when it comes to a group of strangers, they'll freeze up and have a terrible time. The nervous tension that sometimes goes into performing at a social gathering is not unlike the tension you can experience speaking in public, which, as I've said, is more terrifying to most people than death itself.

Social gatherings and public speaking are not, after all, that dissimilar. In both scenarios there's you and a lot of people who, if not actually an "audience," at least *seem* like an audience, not only full of strangers, but also, potential judges (particularly if your negative and slightly paranoid projection system is in gear—which, if you are experiencing any nerves at all, it is).

So, the techniques you would use for public speaking are not unlike those you would use for social gatherings, or even job interviews. Let's face it, a job interview, particularly if you're being interviewed by a committee instead of by only one interviewer, is just another version of public speaking.

So, how do you transform your interviewer from Attila the Hun into your best friend? Personalization.

How do you transform the board meeting table, or even the party buffet, from a battlefield of potential land mines into, let us say, your favorite picnic spread?

Sense Memory.

If it's fried chicken that really turns you on, imagine a big basket of your favorite, most succulent pieces right in the middle of the board meeting table or party buffet. *Smell* that chicken. *Feel* its salty grease on your fingers and face. Imagine you are eating it. *Taste* that doughy, salty, spicy batter on the roof of your mouth and in the corners of your cheeks. Particularly if that chicken goes with a wonderful memory of you picnicking by a waterfall. With or without somebody else. With or without clothes.

Do whatever you need to do to transform any potentially tension-producing scene into a place where you can relax, be yourself, and even have fun. Bring in your favorite Animal, if that'll relax you more than anything else. Or put an Inner Walnut into your chest, and feel your whole self vibrate with its special knowledge.

Brian, a twenty-four-year-old animator who worked with me, knew he had a good sense of humor, but it seemed to disappear when he felt he had to be charming at a party.

When Brian closed his eyes and asked for a symbol of his sense of humor, he saw Bart Simpson. He put the image into his heart, and just feeling it there, reminded him of how good his sense of humor was and gave him the confidence and support he needed to allow it to come out.

If it's Mantras (or affirmations) that relax you, you might think of writing them down on a piece of paper and putting the paper in your pocket for you to feel, to remember its words, whatever they are—"I'm safe," or "I'm okay," or "At least I'm getting a free meal."

You could, of course, instead, have a Magic Stone in that pocket, or a special Prop, maybe even a piece of fried chicken. Although that could get messy and you might end up feeling more, rather than less, self-conscious, if the entire left pocket of your jacket were gradually becoming stained with grease.

Maybe an Inner Monologue about your body will keep you from focusing on the judgments you imagine other people are making about you. Your Inner Monologue might sound something like, "Where am I tense? Is my left shoulder up near my ear? Am I holding tension in my hip joints? Do I have to go to the bathroom?"

The trick is to think anything, just so long as the attention is on you and on your being nice to yourself, instead of on someone who you think might be judging you, but who is probably only wishing he had some fried chicken.

Don't forget, before you go into that difficult party, luncheon, or meeting, to take a moment to check in with how you are really feeling.

IT WORKS FOR ACTORS, IT CAN WORK FOR YOU

If you're pretending to yourself that you're okay and that everything is going to be fine when you're actually feeling scared and that everything will turn out to be a disaster, then your body will be spending a lot of unnecessary energy trying to convince you of what you already know is a lie. Admit how you feel, so you can use that energy for something else, simply for being there and being intelligent, or witty, or yourself as you would be if you weren't in an unconscious war with yourself.

If you have to go to a party with your mother-in-law, and you hate your mother-in-law, admit you hate her. (Probably only to yourself.) If you're at a dinner party with someone whose politics you find repulsive, admit this at least to yourself. If this person happens to be a prospective investor in your company, you may want to keep this to yourself. But at least know it yourself.

If someone at a party does or says something that really ticks you off, you might ask yourself: Am I angry because of something that was done to me as a child, that has nothing to do with the stupidity of the person I seem to hate? If the answer is yes, put the anger where it belongs, in your past, so you can truly be at that party, instead of unconsciously reliving some ancient trauma.

Maybe Playing a Character will work best for you. If you need to feel and appear strong, smart, and "together," try playing John F. Kennedy. A lot of men in my workshops choose him. One woman found that by playing him, she had more authority and felt more alive. Plus her voice automatically lowered and it felt and sounded stronger.

Who has the qualities you feel you need for that family function, sales meeting, or debutante ball? Queen Elizabeth for poise? Zorro for daring? George Washington for power?

TWO TRUE STORIES

BRUCE, A THIRTY-NINE-YEAR-OLD corporate executive, tried playing George Washington at one of my workshops. He found that when he walked around as if he were George Washington, he stood up straighter, his shoulders automatically stayed back and down, and, in fact, his whole posture radically improved.

When Bruce came to a follow-up workshop, he actually said he felt this little exercise had changed his life. I'm always amazed with success stories like these. But then, acting is a magical art.

Bruce said that by walking into a room as George Washington, with his new posture, he noticed not only that he was standing up straighter with his head held high, but that he felt better about himself. He felt stronger, more powerful, like more of a presence, and he thought people noticed this and were treating him with a respect he had never felt before. (Maybe because he was treating himself with more respect than ever before.)

Roger, a thirty-six-year-old CEO of a computer company, came to me because he felt uncomfortable at business functions and social gatherings. Roger told me that he used to love to bite his dog on the neck. (What can I say? This was his idea of fun.)

I suggested he start imagining his dog at business meetings and social functions. He did, and it worked. He feels that dog's neck on his mouth and he starts to smile and relax. He doesn't have to feel himself biting his dog's neck every minute he's there. Sometimes, just imagining his dog in his arms before he goes in can loosen him up for the whole evening.

IT WORKS FOR ACTORS, IT CAN WORK FOR YOU

Often, it's enough for you to simply prepare with whatever acting technique you are going to use at the party and trust that the effect of the exercise will stay with you. It's how most actors prepare for playing a scene. They prepare, and then just go in there and play the scene. If your preparation dries up on you, you can always summon it back when you need it.

If Roger gets tense in the middle of a party, he can always bring his dog back, or lock himself in a bathroom for a little while and do a longer Sense Memory of playing with that silly old dog.

THE LIFE OF THE PARTY

SOME OF MY clients who feel they are not as clever, witty, funny, or as fun to be with as they wish they could be at a party work on playing various comedians. They usually choose Jerry Seinfeld,

Steve Martin, or Robin Williams. And suddenly, their behavior becomes much more spontaneous. Not only do they notice that they're more relaxed, but they find themselves saying funny things. I think it's because if they're open, they're plugging into some great archetypal Comedian Energy.

I figure that's what happened when I played a clown, that I somehow tapped into archetypal Clown Energy. I was playing the Clown Ring Master with Circus Flora and as soon as I saw and felt the white greasepaint on my face, my looping eyebrows, and the red heart on my cheek, I began to be funnier than I ever dreamt I could be. I could only conclude I was allowing some magical archetypal Clown Energy to channel through me. (It sure felt wonderful!)

So don't forget, makeup can also transform your state of being. I'm not advocating that you wear white greasepaint to a party. But I do find that if I'm going somewhere I need to be funny and I wear a little blue mascara on my lashes, I end up being funnier than if I don't wear it.

Maybe a polka dot bow tie will do the trick for you.

Some of my clients find that imagining that they are clowns is all they actually need to have fun at a party. They'll imagine a red rubber ball at the end of their nose, or big floppy shoes on their feet, or even that they're wearing a big clown suit with a thick ruffled collar and cuffs. They'll decide this *before* they go to the party, and this Preparation amuses them, so they're having fun even before as they walk into that party, which can only help them to have fun once they're there. Even if they aren't the most outrageous, amusing center of attention and life of the party that ever was.

Maxine, a twenty-six-year-old architect, found that pretending she was her new little kitten was all she needed to begin to relax and be playful. This was the perfect technique for her to use for her best friend's engagement party, where she knew she would be tense. Obviously, her kitten would not have been as effective for the major presentation she was going to give two days later. Playing an older cat, maybe a puma, might have been more useful there.

28

· So You Want to · Look and Feel Young?

WHAT DOES IT mean to look and feel young? I don't think it always means having less wrinkles as much as it means to have more spontaneity and aliveness, more joy in living, and more curiosity about life—qualities that, in fact, many young children possess.

IT WORKS FOR ACTORS, IT CAN WORK FOR YOU

As you know by now, the techniques in this book are designed to transform you into the most alive self you can be. So, if you care about looking and feeling young, and you're working on the techniques in this book, you're at least halfway there.

Meanwhile, let me address some of the more superficial aspects of looking young, although I do think America loses a lot by not honoring the maturity, depth, and glory of its older citizens over forty. (Okay, okay, I'm over forty.)

So, how did the great English actress Dame Edith Evans, at the age of sixty-five, play the sixteen-year-old Juliet and convince everyone in the audience that she was young, pretty, and really sixteen? How did she get her rave reviews and seem, by all accounts, totally believable as the sixteen-year-old Juliet?

What innocence and openness did she know how to access that could have made her shine on that London stage as if she were a young girl? Maybe it was a Sense Memory she used, or a way of walking. Maybe it was her Inner Monologue, or a song in her head. Or maybe she just surrendered to Playing a Character.

A CHEAP, CHARMING TRICK

HERE'S HOW THE great American actress Katherine Cornell played the sixteen-year-old Juliet when she was well into her forties.

Robert Butman, my drama teacher at college, once visited the great Cornell in her dressing room before she went on stage. As he walked in, he saw her shaking her hands over her head, as if she wanted to shake them off her wrists. He finally asked her what she was doing.

She explained that when she shook her hands over her head, the veins of age disappeared, and her hands literally became smooth and young looking. I tried it. She was right. It works.

Who knows, maybe that was all she needed to convince the rest of her that she *was* young, and then her body would move as if she were young, and her voice sounded more youthful. She would even have been breathing differently, once she had convinced herself that she and her body were young.

If that's all it took, the more power to her. Whatever it takes. Remember?

How else could she have made herself appear younger? The same way any actor might get himself into any character's frame of mind and state of being: by using Imagination, Sense Memory, Props, Substitution, Personalization, Music, Costume, Inner Monologue, Actions, or an Animal Exercise.

DAVID GETS YOUNGER

DAVID, A FORTY-YEAR-OLD owner of a company that manufactured eyeglasses, wanted not only to look and feel younger, but also to recapture the spontaneity and joy he was sure he had felt as a child. For parties, business meetings, and everything else. Our challenge was for him to play the role of his Youthful More Spontaneous Self.

He attacked the role the same way any actor would who needed to play a younger version of a forty-year-old owner of a company that manufactured eyeglasses.

At my suggestion, David made a list of activities that he thought would make him feel and therefore look younger. They included riding on a merry-go-round.

So I suggested David take a ride on a merry-go-round. He did, and had a wonderful time.

Then I asked him to do a Sense Memory of riding on the merry-go-round. He *felt* the wooden horse under him, *saw* and *felt* the brass pole in front of him, *heard* the calliope music, and *felt* himself going up and down and up and down.

He started smiling, and his whole face relaxed. Obviously, he had only good memories of riding on merry-go-rounds when he was a child, and had found a quick way to access his little boy self and all the times he'd ridden free and smiling on a merry-go-round. Somehow, there, he'd always felt safe.

I suggested David do his Sense Memory of riding on the merry-go-round before he went to a party where he might feel uncomfortable, just the way an actor will do a Sense Memory as a preparation before a scene in a movie or a play.

David began to feel at ease at parties in a way he had never felt before. For one thing, he knew he looked better. Somehow, recreating the ride up and down on the merry-go-round made the scowl lines between his eyebrows disappear. In fact, at the mere sound, in his head, of the calliope music, he would start to smile. And if he found himself getting tense, just putting himself back on his blue and brown horse would relax him all over again.

Carrying a balloon also made David smile, especially a helium-filled balloon that he felt could lift him off the ground. Who knows why balloons always make him smile. Maybe people that he loved bought him balloons when he was a kid. But it's always a young smile, and his face relaxes and he somehow becomes more open and trusting. And yes, this is attractive on him.

On his way to what he considers his more creative meetings, where he knows he needs to be particularly inventive, original, and spontaneous, David imagines that he's punching a balloon up in the air, and he'll bounce along with the rhythm of his punches.

What childhood games or activities can *you* remember, to bring you back to your playful, youthful self?

YOU *CAN* LOOK YOUNGER

THE RESULT OF any sensory recreation of an event from your childhood (sensory, of course, so that your body will believe you're really there) is that you will look younger.

Yes, this is amazing. But it works. Try it.

Recreate a birthday party you had when you were five. Be specific about the sensory details:

- ❑ Really *taste* the cake.
- ❑ Really *see* your best girlfriend or boyfriend.
- ❑ *See* your mother, what she's wearing, how she looks.
- ❑ *Hear* her voice.
- ❑ *Feel* her touch your hair or kiss you.
- ❑ Is there music? If there is, *hear* it.
- ❑ *See* the decorations, the balloons, streamers, party favors.
- ❑ Imagine putting a shiny hat on your head, if there were shiny hats, or blowing a noisemaker, if there were noisemakers.
- ❑ Try talking to your mother, your friends, the dog you had then. Or imagine the dog you wished you had had then. See how you feel. Feel how you feel. Be there.

Maybe you'll want to laugh. So laugh. If you want to cry, cry. After you've done the exercise, look in a mirror and see if you don't look just a little bit younger. See if your muscles haven't returned to older patterns, and if the tension around your eyes hasn't relaxed. I'm not saying you can make all your wrinkles go away, but you will probably be surprised by how your face has changed. Try it and see.

29

• Looking and Feeling • Sexy, Romantic, and Gorgeous

KAREN, A FORTY-YEAR-OLD corporate executive, complained that when she came home at night to her husband, it was very hard for her to turn into the soft, feminine, and sexual woman she knew she could be with him, and wanted to be with him. She asked me if I knew of some technique she could use to leave behind what she perceived as the mainly masculine role that she played during the day, a businesswoman in a business suit, along side businessmen, in a man's world.

I suggested that the role she played at the office was no more invalid or unnatural than the one she played in the bedroom. They were both parts of her, important parts of her, and both "natural." A lion is as real and "natural" stalking his prey as he is eating it or sunning with the pride. Animals sometimes go from role to role more easily than some of us humans. Or so it would seem.

I suggested Karen view her Business Self as a role she played no less brilliantly than any actor playing a character that he had researched and knew inside out. It was a role that she had worked hard to get right, and she had been successful.

Karen realized that when she was at work, her walk and movements were slower and more definite than when she felt relaxed and "natural" at home. At work she did indeed have a special script, a special costume, her voice was lower, and her words more measured. Karen only needed help in switching from one role to another.

SWITCHING ROLES

HOW AND WHY is it difficult for some people to go easily from one role to another?

For one thing, a body at rest likes to stay at rest. For another, many people feel comfortable thinking they have a definite and finite identity. Our identity is an invisible essence at best. How could it not feel good to think we truly know who we are for an instant, with a clear and finite definition of who we are? But it's the rare person who's always in touch with his or her identity as Everlasting Light.

Many of us have learned to limit the number of roles we play in order to please the people around us, who want to know that we're one thing and only one thing. How many "grown-ups" do you know who are still stuck playing the good little boy, or the good little girl, probably because their parents couldn't deal with them as anything else, both when they were kids, and when they grew up. And it's not only parents who want other people to "behave," so they can feel they're "in control."

I've met more people than I want to remember who were more comfortable thinking I was either an actress *or* a writer than that I was both. Not to mention a teacher. I know that if I had had only one of these careers, certain people would have felt they had a handle on me, and somehow felt more in control and not overwhelmed. I can't count the number of times I've been told, "Jane, you can only do one thing. And you certainly can only do one thing *well*. So you need to choose. Be an actress *or* a writer. But you can't do both."

Society accepts a certain amount of hyphenating. Mother-teacher, certainly. Director-star-woman is harder—ask Streisand.

My tax accountant once said to me, "Give up your acting and teach. That's where you're making money." I had to look at *who* was telling me to teach and not act. He was a man who had gone into accounting because he wasn't making it as an actor.

And you? What are the sources of your own limited belief systems? If they limit you, can you get rid of them?

Can you see them, see that they're untrue, and let them go? Why not. Sometimes just seeing where we're blocked sets us free. We *can* be more than one thing, play more than one role. We can be more than we think we can be.

I HAD TO GET FIRED TO CHANGE MY ROLE

I THINK I gave away the punch line, but the only way I was able to let go of the role of Lady Anne, who I was playing in Shakespeare's *Richard III* on Broadway was to get fired.

I'll explain. Joseph Papp, founder of the New York Shakespeare Festival, had hired me to play Lady Anne opposite Michael Moriarity's Richard. Actually, I was hired to replace Marsha Mason who had given her notice on opening night.

I rushed into the role. I had only a week to prepare, and Lady Anne's first scene is not only long and hard, but considered by many to be the most difficult scene for an actress in all of Shakespeare.

Lady Anne is following a coffin. She is not happy. Actually, she is crying and cursing. The man in the coffin is her dead father-in-law, a man she loved, whom Richard killed. Richard had also killed her husband, whom she also loved. Anne knows that Richard killed them both. She's not only in mourning, but asking God to torture Richard and kill or maim any children he might have, that sort of thing.

And then Richard comes in, woos her, and asks her to marry him. *In front of the coffin*. And by the end of the scene, she says yes.

Every actress, critic, director, and scholar probably has his own explanation for why she gives in. Maybe it's as simple as her knowing that Richard would kill her, too, if she says no, and she values life more than death. Though let's face it, she's not going to be married to a very nice man, and he ends up killing her anyway.

So what's my point? After six weeks, I got fired. Even though many people who saw me in the role thought I was wonderful, and one of the most moving Lady Annes they'd ever seen. (Even I thought I was good.)

Why was I fired? Maybe Michael Moriarty really wanted to do the play with my understudy. Anyway, that's what he told me. He said it was *his* decision, not Papp's. I think I got fired because I just got carried away with being Lady Anne. And I didn't know how to stop.

Jill Clayburgh told me that the great actress and acting teacher Uta Hagen forbade the actresses in her classes even to work on Lady Anne, because Anne is such a masochist, that her masochism could too easily leak into the life of the actress playing her.

This sort of leakage is not uncommon for actors. During his largely successful career, one of our most brilliant comedians has repeatedly ended up in a mental institution when he couldn't stop himself from thinking he *was* one of the characters he'd invented. It happens. One lets the character in, and is possessed by the character's energy.

Anyway, true or false, I believe it's possible that just as Lady Anne got herself decapitated, I got myself fired. I had simply played her to the hilt, and got carried away. I had become so full of Lady Anne's self-destruction that being fired was the inevitable conclusion of my being immersed in the role.

I never wanted that to happen again. So I had to make sure I had a technique to make that not happen, and I found a number of ways to let go of my characters as soon as the curtain came down.

**IT WORKS FOR ACTORS,
IT CAN WORK FOR YOU**

As in the theater, so it is in life. If there's a role you're playing, know how to let it go as soon as you don't need it anymore.

TECHNIQUES FOR LETTING YOUR CHARACTER GO

LET'S SAY I want to let go of Lady Anne. I close my eyes and see her in my mind. When I can see her (on a screen, in a landscape, wherever), I start to talk to her. And I say good-bye to her. I thank her for being with me. I let her thank me for playing her as well as I could or did. I hear her. Then maybe I imagine we hug. And I'll see her go off to her castle.

Here's another way to let a character go. Change your costume. Now, if I do a play or a movie, I try not to wear the character's clothing home. If I've worn my own clothes in a movie, I'll see the character in a visualization, in those clothes, and watch her disappear, and say good-bye. Then I'll change, before I go home, into something else.

Or I can change my makeup. Many actors make a point of taking their makeup off in the theater. Or on the set. They could do it at home, but then they take the risk of taking the character home with them. So they'll try to take off their makeup *consciously*, as if it were really the character's face that they're removing from their own.

Changing costumes and makeup and visualizing and then saying good-bye to a character are all techniques that Karen could use in her quest to let go of her Business Self when she came home.

KAREN MAKES THE SWITCH

THE CEREMONIES I should have done with Lady Anne and that I now do with any character I should find myself playing are the same I suggested to Karen.

So now, before she takes on the role of Seductive Wife, Karen closes her eyes and sees her Business Self. She might say something to her like, "Thanks for your strength and mental acuity, which I won't need until tomorrow morning. Good-bye for now. Thanks for helping me earn money today, so I can help pay the rent and eat and buy new clothes and see Jane Marla Robbins. Good-bye. Good night."

Then she might hear her Business Self say something like, "Thank *you*. You were smart today, and helped me be clever. We'll do some more good work tomorrow. Good-bye. Good night."

Then Karen would watch her Business Self wave and go off to a special house full of financial statements and business presentations. What's important is that she see her go off *somewhere else*, so that Karen is free to play *another* Karen, a seductive Karen, a softer Karen. She needs to turn off the computer in her head and get into her body. Then she can enjoy the role of Karen the Temptress, the Siren, the Femme Fatale, a role for which she can do a preparation just as an actress might prepare for Cleopatra, Mata Hari, or any other temptress, siren, or femme fatale.

Sometimes, Karen simply changes her costume or her make-up. There are other "character adjustments" Karen sometimes does, some of which she found by answering the questions in the next section.

HOW TO PLAY THE TEMPTRESS, SIREN, AND FEMME FATALE

MAYBE YOU, TOO, want to play the temptress, siren, or femme fatale. Maybe you just want to feel sexy, soft, and seductive. Here are some questions that might help.

Write down your answers, or close your eyes, see your archetypal Seductive Self on a screen, and ask *her* the questions. These are questions any actress might use if she were playing a temptress, siren, or femme fatale:

- ❑ How does your character walk? (For example, does she move her hips more freely than you do?)
- ❑ What does she wear? (Body-revealing silks?)
- ❑ What Sense Memory could you use to make yourself feel soft, sexy, inviting? A first kiss? Someone's hand on your thigh?
- ❑ Would playing an animal loosen you up? How about a lazy cat, silver gray, or Russian blue, languorous and stretching on a bed?
- ❑ What if you imagined that you were sipping the richest cognac in the world? Would this warm you up? Relax you? Loosen you up?
- ❑ Would a sauna turn you on? Remember, you could take a real one, as a Preparation, or recreate one sensorily.
- ❑ What about a warm bath full of aromatic oils or luxurious bubbles? You could prepare with a real one, or recreate one sensorily.
- ❑ What about a massage—real or imaginary. Maybe there's some special smelling oil that turns you on. For Karen it was patchouli. She both uses it as a Sense Memory, and has a little bottle handy.
- ❑ Maybe there's a song that makes you feel sultry. Maybe it's a song Marlene Dietrich sings.
- ❑ Maybe it's Playing Marilyn Monroe, imagining you have her body and are wearing the same dress or slip she wore in a particular movie.
- ❑ Marlene Dietrich actually designed her own glamorous image (hair, eyebrows, lips, and makeup). How could you design your own?
- ❑ Is there a special food that turns you on? Oysters? Peanut butter? Whatever works for you.

- ❏ What if you painted your nails (hopefully, with time to let them dry before hitting the sheets)?
- ❏ And what about the sheets? (Now of course, you're designing your set, and finding your Props.) Will satin sheets make you feel sexier than cotton? Or will they make you afraid you'll slide off the bed?
- ❏ Would a sexy painting in your Inner Walnut help you? Or imagining it on the wall opposite your bed? Maybe an Indian painting of people making love, in sensual, outrageous positions. Maybe three people. Maybe four.
- ❏ You can, of course, ask for help from your mate. The two of you could improvise a scene. If you're female maybe it would turn you on to be a medieval Damsel in Distress, rescued by a Knight in Shining Armor. This is particularly effective if your mate is turned on by being the Knight. The two of you could go as far as you wanted, have medieval hors d'oeuvres in bed together. Or a suit of armor. Or a horse. Whatever turns you on.

HOW MEN CAN LOOK AND FEEL SEXY

OKAY MEN. TRY answering the questions Karen answered in the section above (with a few judicious changes, of course), and the ones below:

- ❏ Would you feel sexier if you imagined you were George Clooney? Sean Connery? Antonio Banderas?
- ❏ What clothing makes you feel sensual? A scratchy sweater, or a soft one?
- ❏ Is there an animal you could play that would bring out your animal feelings? Black panthers work for some people, snakes, for others. What if you played a rambunctious dog? What works for *you*?
- ❏ Do you prefer candlelight?

- ❑ How does your Sexy Self walk? Is your chest lifted, your mouth relaxed?
- ❑ How does your Sexy Self talk? Slower than you usually do? Does the voice have a more velvet timbre?
- ❑ What activities turn you on—reading poetry, walking in nature, betting on horses? Remember, you can either do these or imagine you are doing them.
- ❑ What Sense Memory could you use to make yourself feel sexy? Maybe you have a hot memory from long ago.
- ❑ Does looking at your bankbook turn you on?
- ❑ What about baseball? How would you feel if you remembered your favorite hero hitting a home run, and you heard the fans cheering?
- ❑ What if *you* had hit the home run and they were cheering for *you*?
- ❑ Would an Inner Mantra help, like "It's safe to be sexy," or "It's fun to be sexy," or "I am sexy."
- ❑ Maybe music turns you on. Either actual music, or music you hear in your head, in case the music that turns *you* on doesn't happen to turn on the person you're romancing. Maybe there's a special song. Maybe it's Julio Iglesias singing "To All the Girls I've Loved Before." Maybe it's you singing "To All the Girls I've Loved Before." Maybe it's playing Julio Iglesias singing "To All the Girls I've Loved Before." Maybe Julio Iglesias turns you on. Whatever works.

PUTTING MORE ROMANCE IN YOUR RELATIONSHIP

ROMANCE CAN BE just the thing to keep a relationship, and the people in it, excited, happy, and alive.

Try using Imagination and Improvisation to keep it in *your* relationship. Joe Bologna and Renee Taylor are actors and writers, and have been married to each other for almost forty years. They wrote and starred in the film *Made For Each Other,* as wonderful and funny a romantic comedy as I've ever seen. In their personal life, Joe and Renee sometimes invent and improvise scenes to keep romance in their relationship, and they have one of the sturdiest marriages I know.

Here's a scene they told me about. They arranged to meet at a fancy hotel, but they agreed beforehand that they would pretend they didn't know each other. So she was wandering around the lobby, and he came up to her, and asked her name and pretended to pick her up. She played hard to get, as long as she could, but eventually, they ended up renting a room in the hotel and having a wonderful time.

Would a romantic improvisation spice up *your* relationship? Here are some premises that may work for you, or maybe they'll inspire you to think up some of your own:

- ❏ South American gaucho meets shy cantry girl in airport. They share a passionate love of tapas and electric eye contact.
- ❏ American architect visiting in Paris has been following a mysterious stranger for an hour, attracted by some specific part of her anatomical architecture . . .

You could imagine you are the romantic leads from such classics as *Casablanca, Romeo and Juliet,* and *Titanic*.

When you've finished playing your invented characters and go back to being yourselves, you may be surprised by how you and your partner look at each other, and by the imagination, romance, and even passion that you see in each other.

30

• You *Can* Change • How You Act

THE TECHNIQUES IN this book are designed to help you change how you act. Changing isn't always easy. Changing behavior that's taken us years to perfect can be hard.

What behaviors did you buy this book to try and change? Tenseness? Shyness? Hiding parts of yourself, instead of being all you could be?

Few changes happen overnight, although some of the people who work with me do get some very fast results.

Some acting techniques take some people longer to "master" than others. Stanislavsky did say that it takes twenty years to make an actor.

Don't be hard on yourself if you don't get it all right away. If you were learning to lift weights, you wouldn't expect yourself to lift a hundred pounds without first starting with five, and then ten. You may need to work out daily. For some people, repetition is important.

And don't think that just because you've used a technique once and a situation that had been difficult before is suddenly a breeze, that it will be as easy the next time if you don't use the technique.

If you find that changing how you act is particularly hard, you might ask yourself the following questions:

- ❏ Who won't love me if I'm strong?
- ❏ Do I think they'll hate me, or worse, abandon me to die?
- ❏ Do I feel I deserve to be happy? If not, why not?
- ❏ What do I risk to lose if I'm powerful? What do I risk to gain?
- ❏ Who told me I couldn't perform well? Could that person have been wrong?
- ❏ Can I admit they might have been wrong?
- ❏ Would they be angry, thinking I thought they were wrong?
- ❏ Will *I* be okay if I admit that they're wrong?
- ❏ Did someone program me to perform brilliantly, who couldn't love me just for "being," so that I'm daring that person to love me if I fail, since I'm angry and afraid that they would only love me if I were a success? Is it possible that that person could never love herself or himself, and so could never love me, no matter *what* I did? Is it possible I don't have to fail for that person's love, since he or she never had it to give, anyway?

Invent your own questions. Find your own answers, and know you are not alone.

I, for one, will certainly not hate you if you change. And more important, you might really come to respect and love yourself.

31

• Playing Your • Ideal Self

Now for the role of a lifetime: You.

How do you play you? You as you want to be. You as you want to see yourself, in any situation where you want to look, feel, and behave in a certain way, a way you're possibly not used to looking, feeling, and behaving. Do you think that any of these parts of you need help:

- ❑ Your Most Alive Self
- ❑ Your Most Gracious and Successful Host Self
- ❑ Your Brilliant Public Speaker Self
- ❑ Your Effortlessly Fluent Writer Self
- ❑ Your Disciplined Athletic Self
- ❑ Your Most Dynamic Teacher Self
- ❑ Your Saner Shopper Self
- ❑ Your Whole and Self-Confident Self

Here's one of the techniques that actors use when they're Playing a Character. The first time I heard about this technique was at one of Donna Gerard's acting classes. Donna's students included Marlon Brando and Bruce Dern.

Donna basically taught us a visualization technique. First, we were to close our eyes and relax, and once we were in this semi-meditative state, she asked us to *see* the character we were working on—Ophelia, Don Juan, whoever. The idea was to speak to the character and have the character answer.

For the *Rocky* movies, Talia Shire spoke to the shy, now famous Adrian, and Adrian answered, showing the actress how she walked, sat, dressed, and talked. For her role in *The Godfather* movies, Talia watched her character show her not only how to be in various scenes in the movie, but also how she had been in various scenes of her life that weren't in the script. (When actors know this kind of detail about their characters, their performances are often deeper and more convincing than if they don't.)

If, in life, you have a "difficult role" to play, whether it's Charismatic Speech Giver, or Hostess with the Mostest, you can ask that part of you for answers in the same way.

STEVE'S MACHO SELF

STEVE, A THIRTY-THREE-YEAR-OLD psychology professor, was upset that women seemed to see him as "soft, a pushover, only the good friend, instead of the jock." He told me that he wanted to appear "more masculine."

He did, in fact, have a very soft side that was extremely evident.

I asked Steve to close his eyes, and to invite his most masculine, macho self to appear. This self would be a combination not only of all Steve's macho energies, but also, possibly, even archetypal Machismo.

When Steve closed his eyes, he saw an open, grassy field in front of him. Finally a figure appeared, a muscled kind of Mike

Macho that only vaguely resembled Steve. I asked Steve to talk to the image, to ask him what Steve needed to do in his life so he could really own some of his characteristics.

"Exercise," said the macho guy.

It turned out that Steve didn't exercise at all, which is why his body was a little flabby. Flaccid, actually. It had never occurred to me to mention this, for fear of offending him and making him feel even more insecure about his "masculinity" and how he looked. But when an image from his own psyche started telling him to "exercise," I figured I could jump in.

"Ask him what kind of exercise he wants you to do," I said.

Steve asked and his macho self answered, "Walk every day."

This was, of course, an answer that I could not have come up with, not knowing the limits of Steve's body, or what he could or wouldn't do. I asked Steve if he could and would do this.

He said yes.

Then I asked Steve to ask the figure what else he wanted Steve to do. The figure asked him to buy a special red crew neck sweater and to eat more Mexican food.

Whatever works.

Why this strengthened Steve's macho energy I don't know. I don't care. What I love is that the answers came not from me, but from Steve, from deep inside, where he somehow knew what he needed to balance himself.

Later, I had Steve play his Macho Self: "Mike Macho." I asked Steve to exaggerate Mike's posture, voice, and feelings. I also had him play his Weak Passive Self, and asked him to exaggerate that self's posture, voice, and feelings.

Then I suggested there was a self somewhere in the middle who, like Steve, could be not only centered, strong, compassionate, smart, and generous, but also as "masculine" as any man needed to be. It took a little convincing, but finally Steve understood.

Steve began to talk to this Centered Self in meditation. Then he played him, acting out his posture, voice, and feelings.

Soon Steve attracted women who wanted him to be more than their best friend. . . .

BONNIE PLAYS HER IDEAL SELF

BONNIE WAS FORTY-EIGHT years old and owned a successful ad agency. When she came to me, she was looking for the courage to leave her agency, in order to give seminars to help people start their own businesses. This was something she knew about. Twenty years earlier, she had started her own business from scratch.

But Bonnie was scared. She didn't know where to start, and mainly had trouble seeing herself being as strong, wise, and charismatic as she thought a seminar leader should be.

I asked her to close her eyes and see herself leading her ideal seminar. I asked her how she looked. I asked her what she was wearing.

She saw herself looking confident and standing tall. She was wearing a mauve suit with simple pearl earrings.

I asked her to describe her outfit in as many details as possible.

She saw a high-collared silk blouse that went with the suit. There was a pin on her lapel, and she was wearing a pair of tan shoes. She understood the exercise, and began to describe the shape of the pin, and the cut of the shoes.

I asked her to talk to this Ideal Seminar Leader, to ask her for "acting tips," in a sense, on how to play her in her real life. Did she, for example, want Bonnie to buy a mauve suit?

Bonnie's Seminar Leader said yes. And a high-collared blouse, and tan shoes, as well. And the earrings and the pin.

I asked if she wanted Bonnie to do anything else so she could become more present in Bonnie's life.

She said she wanted Bonnie to start going to a gym to get into shape. She told her to stop eating wheat, but to eat more asparagus and beets. She told her to take singing lessons. Not all at once, mind you, but in her own good time.

Bonnie was amazed. These were things she had thought about, but she had never really heard a voice loud enough, either inside of herself or out, telling her to do them. Now she was motivated. And it certainly wasn't me telling her what to do; it was Bonnie herself.

Slowly, Bonnie began to do the things that her Ideal Seminar Leader suggested. She bought the suit, she changed her diet. She joined a gym.

Now came the issue of the workshop itself. Bonnie hadn't a clue where to begin. She asked her Ideal Seminar Leader Self what she should do.

The answer was loud and clear. "You already know how to do it, just watch me."

When Bonnie had first told me about the seminars she dreamed of giving, she was sure she wanted to teach only women. But when she saw her ideal seminar, in meditation, she was surprised to see not only women, but also several men.

And at the end of the workshop, one of the men came up to her and thanked her for giving him the courage, finally, to start his own business.

I think it was this image, and how good it made her feel, that finally gave her the courage to start her own seminars.

PLAYING THE ROLES IN YOUR LIFE TO THE HILT

ARE THERE ROLES in *your* life that you feel could be easier, maybe more productive, maybe, even fun?

You could start with the family roles. Maybe you're having trouble being Mother, Daughter, Father, or Son.

Sometimes, all you have to do is visualize, in meditation, your Ideal Loving Mother Self or Ideal Loving Daughter (or Father, Uncle, Brother), and ask the part of you that you have visualized what you need to do in your life in order to play that role more easily, and to the best of your ability.

It's sometimes easiest to see these characters if you put yourself in a specific, sensorily created place first—maybe in a green field, as Steve did, or maybe in a theater, so you can ask your character to appear on the stage. Or maybe in a cave. The trick here is to have your body feel the physical realities of the place—the texture of the grass in the field, the cushion on the seat in the theater, the coolness of the stone in the cave. Giving your body this sensory input seems to help some people to leave the physical realm and to travel deep inside where there are other realities, such as the archetypal images you will be summoning.

Once you have found your character, try asking him or her the following questions:

- ❑ What should I wear so you can be more fully in my life?
- ❑ Are there any special foods I should eat? Any I should avoid?
- ❑ Is there any piece of clothing I should add to my wardrobe? Any special colors? Any special jewelry I should be wearing?
- ❑ Are there any special vitamins I should be taking?
- ❑ Is there any special exercise I should be doing?
- ❑ Are there certain people I should be seeing more of (so they can be more fully in my life)?
- ❑ Are there certain people I should be seeing less of, or not at all?
- ❑ Are there any changes I should make to the place where I am living? Should I add a plant or paint a wall?
- ❑ Is there any special advice you can give me about—whatever the issue is: making business presentations, feeling comfortable at parties, and so forth.

See that archetype, and let him or her tell you what you need to do. Maybe that inner part will ask you to stop talking to your father for a while, so that you can get clear about what you like about your relationship, and what part of it may be unbearable.

Maybe you'll only be told to eat asparagus. There may be some vitamin, mineral or other aspect of asparagus that your body needs. (Among other things, asparagus is a diuretic.) It's amazing what we can allow ourselves to see and know when we're relaxed. It's amazing how many answers are actually inside us all the time.

When I was afraid I couldn't write a full-length play all by myself, but I thought I wanted to, one of my teachers, Edwin Steinbrecher, told me to go into meditation and ask my wise Inner Writer what I needed to do so I could write the play. This writer didn't look at all like me, but instead like a dancer out of a painting by Toulouse-Lautrec. She gave me a long list of things to do. I was supposed to collect all the plays, poems, and articles I had written up until then, and put them in a pile on my desk. I was supposed to put plants in my bathroom. And wear boots when writing.

Weird as some of the list sounded, I did everything on it.

And then I sat down and wrote the play. All by myself. (It was *Jane Avril,* and not only was it produced in New York, it was even translated into Danish and performed in Copenhagen.)

Maybe talking to one of your own underdeveloped selves will help *you*. If visualization is not your most accessible talent, you might try writing a dialogue between you and that Ideal Self. Ideally, you'll be doing a kind of automatic writing: you'll write, and then somehow the character will write back. So had I written to my Ideal Writer, the dialogue might have looked something like this:

Me: "Is there anything special I should be eating?"

Ideal Writer: "Spinach."

Me: "Is there any special advice you can give me about writing by myself?"

Ideal Writer: "Wear boots.

Me: "Why?"

Ideal Writer: "They will ground you."

See what works best for you. You may be surprised by what you get.

32

• Now Go Out There • and Have Fun

DESPITE THE FAST, fun world of advertising, a lot of people come to me complaining that there is not enough fun in their lives. It seems that in America, the notion of having fun is still, in certain circles, in disrepute.

Even though the Bible, the most widely read book in America, says, "Clap your hands and make a joyful noise" and "Sing onto the Lord a new song," many people still have difficulty having a good time.

Our founding fathers even wrote it into the Constitution of the United States of America, giving every citizen "certain inalienable rights, among them life, liberty, and the pursuit of *happiness*."

Many people who come to me are either consciously or unconsciously scared to have a good time. Maybe they were yelled at as children when they were having fun. Maybe because their parents didn't know how to have fun themselves, and taught them, by example, that the only way to live is through hard work and suffering.

Having fun is synonymous with feeling good. And most people, when they're feeling good and having fun, perform as well as they possibly can.

Until having fun once again becomes instinctive for you, because we're all born with an instinct for having an outrageously good time, some of the techniques in this book may be just what you need to have a good time.

If you're not used to having fun, don't expect to catch on all at once. Maybe start out having fun for only a few minutes a day. Then increase the dosage, gradually, until you get used to the feeling.

The ability to have fun is a talent like any other. If you don't use it, you lose it.

So how do you practice having fun?

Dig up your list of Sense Memories that make you smile or, better still, giggle. Take out your list of Personalizations and Substitutions and practice being with those people, places, and things that make it easy for you to have fun.

Try feeling the Inner Walnut at your heart, maybe this time with a symbol of your sense of humor. Mine, once, believe it or not, was a madly scrambling Bugs Bunny, and when I discovered him, I really did begin having more fun.

Maybe playing a ridiculously silly clown with big, floppy red shoes will do it for you. Or you might imagine that you have Harpo Marx's outrageous horn in your hand, and you could honk it whenever you wanted.

Maybe there's a funny limerick that gets you grinning. Then hear it in your head.

Everything's game.

See what *you* can find to beef up your pleasure if you're not having enough fun. Every technique in this book can be used to help you to have a good time.

ACTORS NEED TO HAVE FUN, TOO

WHAT DOES AN actor do when he or she has to have fun in a play or a movie?

The versatile actress Elissa Celli had to look as if she were having fun at a party with Lindsay Wagner in the television movie *Street Smarts*. She knew exactly which Sense Memory to use to get herself there. She recreated her experience of being at Rio de Janeiro at Carnival, where she always has fun. She loves the music and the dancing, she loves the people all around her, shouting and singing and having a good time.

She *heard* the music in her head, and *felt* her body dancing. She *heard* the people, and *felt* them next to her. And, if you ever see that party scene in *Street Smarts*, you bet she's having fun.

The wonderful actor Steve Raillsback had a scene in the movie *Armed And Dangerous* where he had to look like he was having fun. Steve was playing "a weird guy on speed" who drove an eight-wheeler, and when John Candy got in his truck, they were supposed to look like they were having a rollicking good time.

Steve happened to be playing a cowboy, and thought he'd imagine himself on a bucking bronco. This, he says, for whatever reason, made him have the best time ever.

JORDAN LEARNS HOW TO HAVE FUN

JORDAN, A TWENTY-SEVEN-YEAR-OLD architect, had trouble going to parties where there were people he didn't know. He had trouble talking, tensed up, and wasn't "himself."

Well, who else, you may well ask, was he, then? Okay, he was his Tense Self.

I asked Jordan if he had ever been relaxed at a social gathering.

Yes, he said, in the old days, when he used to get drunk.

I asked him to remember a time when he had been drunk and full of words.

He remembered being at a bar back in England, when he was still in school. I asked him to recreate the bar, and feel himself drinking whatever he would have been drinking. I asked him what he saw, and who was there.

He remembered Joe, a fellow student, who used to get drunk and be outrageous. Jordan started smiling.

I asked him how Joe would be outrageous.

Jordan remembered Joe getting down on the floor, on his knees, and kissing the shoes of any woman he found attractive. Then he'd go on and on about how she was the most beautiful woman he'd ever seen.

Jordan was having such a good time remembering this, his whole body relaxed. (Actually, I thought it was pretty funny, too.)

Then we worked on the wine he'd been drinking in the bar. Slowly, sensorily, Jordan recreated getting a little drunk, just tipsy enough for his body to relax and feel uninhibited.

"Feel the glass in your hand," I began. "Feel the smoothness of the glass. Feel its weight. Smell the wine. Feel the glass on your lips, and the wine in your mouth. How does it taste? Is it a thick wine? Velvety? Smooth? Is there an edge to it? Can you feel it making your esophagus warm? Your stomach? Your blood vessels? Do your limbs feel heavy, like they've got cement in them?"

I am not suggesting you go out and get drunk in order to be more at ease in social situations. I'm simply saying that if getting drunk was something that has made it easier for you to be with people and have fun, then know that with Sense Memory, you can *control* getting drunk, without the side effects. You'll be able to drive safely, your words won't slur, and you won't be stupid—although you may feel a buzz. If you use Sense Memory, *you* control the effects of the alcohol on your body. The alcohol doesn't control you.

Soon Jordan and I were laughing, seemingly uncontrollably, as if we had really been drinking. We both found this slightly hard to believe, but it was true. And we were having fun.

Jordan was also speaking just a little louder than he usually did, which was also a good thing, because sometimes he tended to talk so softly that I had trouble hearing him. He was loosening up, and he found it was easier for him to talk than it usually was.

Not bad for an imaginary glass of Bordeaux.

NANCY GOES TO THE SUPERMARKET

NANCY, A FIFTY-NINE-YEAR-OLD social worker, was living with a man whose back had suddenly gone into spasms. He could hardly walk. He certainly couldn't go out and buy the groceries, which had been his responsibility before his back went out.

It was bad enough that Nancy suddenly felt she was doing everything for him and nothing for herself. (Well, she was doing a lot more for him than she had been before, like a lot of fetching and carrying and cooking.) But she really hated the shopping. Somehow, going down those supermarket aisles and picking out those groceries felt like indentured slavery to her, and more punishment than she could bear.

I asked Nancy what in her life was really fun for her.

Nancy loved to dance, and was even part of a Scandinavian folk dance group that gave regular public performances. I suggested that she try to dance her way down the supermarket aisles. Not necessarily to make a spectacle of herself, so that people would point and stare, but so that she would feel she was doing something that she loved. Dancing. I reminded her that she could be subtle about it, hear the music only in her head, and only imperceptibly suggest the actual steps.

I suggested she decide on one specific dance, and she chose the tango.

I asked her what her fantasy costume might be. Her task, of course, was to come up with as many sensory details as possible. She fantasized a tight-fitting, long-sleeved, red satin dress with a slit up one side of the skirt. I suggested that when she went shopping, she imagine she was wearing the red satin dress, instead of the blouse and slacks she might actually be wearing.

"Feel the thick, soft satin against your skin," I said, "and the skirt flapping against your legs where the slit is."

But we didn't stop there. She realized it would also be fun to imagine luxurious red roses in her hair and one in her mouth.

I suggested she could even play Carmen Zapata, or any other dancer, if that would make her step lighter and allow her to have more fun.

Then I asked her to imagine that her perfect tango partner might always be around the next aisle. Why shouldn't he be near the string beans and cauliflower?

Shopping suddenly became not only bearable, but even a wonderful kind of game for her. And when her boyfriend's back finally did heal, at least she'd found a way to make her shopping fun.

THE FINAL LESSON OF THIS BOOK

I HOPE YOU'VE tried at least some of the acting techniques in this book, seen how they work, seen how they can change how you feel and behave, and seen that they can even work well. All of them can be used to make you look and feel terrific in situations where you may have been uncomfortable or even miserable before.

Now you know how to prepare for any situation as an actor would.

So put down your book and go out and have fun.

• Acknowledgments •

I HAVE BEEN able to teach only because I have been taught. I am grateful to all of my teachers, especially Martha Graham, John Lehne, Walter Lott, Sonia Moore, Pat Randall, Sandra Seacat, and Edwin Steinbrecher. My students have also been my teachers, and I am deeply grateful to every single one of them.

I have my editor, Mathew Lore, to thank for his belief in this book, and for his invaluable input, and Sue McCloskey, for her help in clarifying and sculpting it.

I have been able to write this book also because of the support and love that both it and I have received from Terry Belanger, Anna Norberg, Bonnie Loren, Pamela Shaw, Rachel Choderov, Dianne Demailly, Patricia Bosworth, Casey Kelly, Ahmed Aboudan, Rob Gardinier, Danny Selznick, Sonny Shear, Dolly Gordon, David Bockoff, Bill Bassett, Eileen Peterson, Phyllis Persechini, Gabrielle Lamirand, Talia Shire, Leon Schneiderman, Judith P. Zinsser, my agent Julia Lord, my sister Aileen Robbins, and my niece Ariel Friedman, who sent me the following message after one of my performances, words that I wish we could all hear all the time: "I knew you could do it; and you did. Just believe. I do."